Praise for *Goliath Must Fall*

Goliath Must Fall will ignite your desire to see your giants defeated and to step into all God has for you.

—CHRISTINE CAINE
FOUNDER, A21 AND
PROPEL WOMEN

Louie Giglio gently invites us to listen to the voice of the Shepherd, who "sets our hearts free." This book will encourage and inspire you.

—RAVI ZACHARIAS
AUTHOR AND SPEAKER

I had a major giant in my life called "fear." If you are battling that same giant, then *Goliath Must Fall* is a must-read.

—SADIE ROBERTSON
AUTHOR, SPEAKER,
ACTOR, AND FOUNDER
OF LIVE ORIGINAL

I believe God is going to set people free of their giants through the wonderful truth Louie shares in this book.

—DR. CHARLES STANLEY SENIOR PASTOR, FIRST BAPTIST ATLANTA PRESIDENT, IN TOUCH MINISTRIES

Great players have had great coaches. Louie helps us understand that God has provided the ultimate coach to help us be victorious over our Goliaths.

—STAN SMITH CHAIRMAN OF STAN SMITH EVENTS, FORMER #1 RANKED TENNIS PLAYER, AND FACE OF THE ICONIC "STAN SMITH SHOE"

Louie is masterful at connecting people with the message of the gospel.

—BRIAN HOUSTON GLOBAL SENIOR PASTOR AND FOUNDER, HILLSONG CHURCH

Louie walks us toward the road to redemption through godly wisdom and relatable transparency.

—LECRAE GRAMMY-AWARD WINNING ARTIST, SONGWRITER, AND PRODUCER

Goliath *Must* Fall

OTHER BOOKS BY LOUIE GIGLIO

The Comeback

Waiting Here for You

Passion: The Bright Light of Glory

Indescribable

I Am Not But I Know I Am

The Air I Breathe

Goliath
Must
Fall

Winning the Battle Against Your Giants

Louie Giglio

W Publishing Group

An Imprint of Thomas Nelson

Published in Nashville, Tennessee, by W Publishing Group, an imprint of Thomas Nelson.

W Publishing Group and Thomas Nelson are registered trademarks of HarperCollins Christian Publishing, Inc.

Thomas Nelson titles may be purchased in bulk for educational, business, fund-raising, or sales promotional use. For information, please e-mail SpecialMarkets@ThomasNelson.com.

Any Internet addresses, phone numbers, or company or product information printed in this book are offered as a resource and are not intended in any way to be or to imply an endorsement by Thomas Nelson, nor does Thomas Nelson vouch for the existence, content, or services of these sites, phone numbers, companies, or products beyond the life of this book.

Unless otherwise noted, Scripture quotations are taken from the Holy Bible, New International Version®, NIV®. Copyright © 1973, 1978, 1984, 2011 by Biblica, Inc.™ Used by permission of Zondervan. All rights reserved worldwide. www.zondervan.com. The "NIV" and "New International Version" are trademarks registered in the United States Patent and Trademark Office by Biblica, Inc.™

Scripture quotations marked ESV are taken from the ESV® Bible (The Holy Bible, English Standard Version®), copyright © 2001 by Crossway, a publishing ministry of Good News Publishers. Used by permission. All rights reserved.

Scripture quotations marked CEV are taken from the Contemporary English Version. Copyright © 1991, 1992, 1995 by American Bible Society. Used by permission.

Scripture quotations marked NKJV are taken from the New King James Version®. © 1982 by Thomas Nelson. Used by permission. All rights reserved.

Scripture quotations marked NLT are taken from the *Holy Bible*, New Living Translation. © 1996, 2004, 2007, 2013 by Tyndale House Foundation. Used by permission of Tyndale House Publishers, Inc., Carol Stream, Illinois 60188. All rights reserved.

Library of Congress Control Number: 2017903611

ISBN 978-0-7180-8888-0 (eBook)
ISBN 978-0-7180-8886-6 (trade paper)

Printed in the United States of America

17 18 19 20 21 LSC 12

Contents

Your Giant *Is* Going Down

The king ducked his head, shuffled outside his tent, and stared at the far hill that lay just outside his war camp. His breakfast settled in an uneasy stomach. All over the valley, the clank of cooking pots could be heard as men lit fires and munched on bread and cheese. It wouldn't be long now until the shouter's voice came again. The king let out a deep sigh.

"How many days does this make?" he asked his aide.

"Forty, sir," came the reply. A ring of guards stood watch around the king's tent. The aide needn't have bothered answering, except his life depended on giving the correct answer to the king. But both the aide and the king knew that King Saul was already aware of the number.

"Can you see him coming?" the king asked.

The aide squinted, shaded his brow, and nodded. "Right on time, sir."

The king grumbled as he slipped into his royal robes, then went silent. His shoulders slumped.

"YOU!" boomed a shout from across the valley. "Why don't you line up for battle today . . . or are you too afraid?" All the soldiers in the Israelite camp turned to watch, many trembling. The taunt was nothing new, but the soldiers took no action. They received no commands. There were no orders to follow. There were no volunteers. They couldn't turn their eyes away, and they hated who stood in front of them, but none of them were brave enough to try and stop him.

The shouter was a brute of a man. Hairy and ugly and foul. Scarred and weathered from a hundred previous battles. A bronze helmet rested on his head. A massive coat of scale armor covered his body. Bronze plates protected his legs. A bronze javelin was slung on his back. The shouter gripped a spear shaft thicker than a weaver's rod, and his shield bearer stood before him, grinning as he relished the fight. With that amount of armor on the brute, the archers likely wouldn't be able to penetrate his defenses. And with an entire army behind him, swordsmen couldn't rush him. Spearmen and charioteers couldn't get close enough before they would be wiped out. The giant was impenetrable. Undefeatable. And no one knew that better than the giant himself.

"You bunch of babies!" the giant called forth. "Am I not a Philistine, and are you not the servants of King Saul? Let's have a contest for men! Same one I proposed yesterday. You choose a man. We'll choose a man. The two men will fight. Whoever wins the battle wins the war. I'll be the man for our side. Who do you have on yours?" He laughed with a long and loud cackle. The giant already knew the answer. No one was going to stand up to him. Jeers and catcalls came from the Philistine camp.

The aide glanced at King Saul. "Sir, any reply for Goliath *today*?" The aide's voice hinted at the significance of the last word.

The king ignored the question. No, there was no reply *today*. There was no reply yesterday, nor had there been the day before that, nor the day before that. The aide knew this. There had been no reply all week, and no reply the week before that, and no reply nearly six weeks ago when this whole debacle started. There was no reply, because nobody in the Israelite army could defeat this giant, and everyone in the Israelite camp knew it. No one knew that better than King Saul himself, the tallest, strongest, and most experienced warrior in the entire Israelite army.

"So that's a 'no' then?" Goliath yelled. "Or is that just the sound of birds chirping I hear?" He spit on the ground and added, "You're worthless! The whole lot of you. Powerless. Weak. Just like your God. I defy you, and I defy your God. Until you're ready to fight like men . . . See you tomorrow, chumps." With that, Goliath and his shield bearer turned on their heels and strode back to their camp.

King Saul cast an extended sidelong glance at his aide. Saul already knew the answer to his own next question even before he asked it: "You've searched everywhere in camp for the strongest fighters, right? How much is the reward up to now?"

"Great wealth," the aide muttered. The king and his aide went through the same checklist every day.

"Anything else?"

"No taxes for the soldier's family."

"Right. Have we forgotten anything?"

The aide cleared his throat. "Your daughter in marriage, sir. The soldiers all know she's part of the deal."

The king sighed again. He looked at the ground and said, "Carry on then." He turned around and shuffled back inside his tent.

Defeated for one more day.

Finding the Right Title

———

Plenty of us face a similar predicament every day—although we're not fighting literal giants. We're facing some sort of insurmountable challenge or problem that rips into our lives. Maybe it's fear. Maybe it's an addiction. Maybe it's anger. Maybe it's the feeling of rejection, a feeling that permeates so many areas of life. Maybe it's the sneaky giant of complacency.

Have you ever felt like King Saul and the Israelite army did? Some kind of giant stands before you, taunting you, harassing you, insulting you. Day after day this giant robs you of your power. You've tried any number of approaches to stop the taunts, but you feel immobilized. Held back. Slowed or stopped from moving forward in a healthy way. Ultimately, you know you're not living the kind of life you want to live. If this is part of your story, then this book is for you.

Our first response is often a quick "no."

"I don't have any Goliaths in my life. I'm in my lane, doing my thing. Living my life."

Some of you would say the opposite. You grabbed this book because you know you have a giant staring you down and you want to know how to defeat it. Yet it's likely all of us have something lurking nearby that's stealing our joy. A habit or a memory or a way of thinking we've grown accustomed to.

It doesn't have to be alcoholism or anorexia or depression. Giants come in all shapes and sizes, some subtle and others stark. The good news is it's not God's plan for you to live with *anything* standing in the middle of your life, demoralizing you day by day by day. These giants harm you and rob God of his glory in your life. God wants you to live free. God wants your giants to fall. He wants you to live without the chains that bind you, unfettered from beliefs that limit you. And you can!

No matter how many times you've tried before or how loud the voice is that says you'll never be different than you are, God says something else today. *You. Can. Live. Free.*

The pages ahead are not just filled with "pie in the sky" optimism. This book is a time-tested pathway for how your life can be different. I know, because I've been there. I've come face-to-face with giants of my own and experienced God's power and strength that surpasses my best efforts. In the chapters to come, I'm going to share from that experience as we carve open the biblical story of David and Goliath. Through that story you'll discover some tools and new habits, some new perspectives, a fresh way of walking through life. The plan toward freedom is doable and straightforward. It invites your success. But first we need to realize that it's not a simple wish that your giant will fall someday, some time. No. It's a *mandate*.

Goliath *must* fall.

Obviously, that's the title of this book, and each word of the title is deliberate—particularly the middle word. We kicked around this title for a long time and chose it purposefully because it underscores a significant God-idea that is important for you and me. By God-idea I mean a foundational theological principle. But don't let the word *theological* throw you off. Think of it like the frame of your house. Some beams or boards are bigger than others and bear more weight. The underlying idea here is a huge beam that anchors God's thoughts about your life and his reputation on earth. The premise is that Jesus' desire for your life and my life is that we would have life to the full. As a result, Jesus will get glory from our lives as the Provider of the very best.

If God has it his way, we live free and he gets glory for being the giant-killer.

We kicked around the idea that maybe we should title the book something different, because much of the big idea we discuss in this book is that Goliath *has already* fallen. Past tense. The same is true of all our giants. The real work is already done by Christ, and Jesus has already taken down all the foes we face in our life. So, we thought, maybe the title should be *Goliath Has Fallen.*

Someone else suggested the title *Goliath Will Fall.* A future hope. Because even though Christ has done the ultimate work, there's still work for us to do. That title is hopeful and faith-filled, looking to the future. Something good is going to happen.

But we stuck with the idea that the clearest title includes the mandate

Goliath *Must* Fall

It's the title that has the fuel inside of it. It's the one that says, "There's a giant in my life that's standing over me, and it's got to go down. Now. Today. Not ten or twenty years in the future. But in the immediate now. In fact, my giant has already been defeated because of what Christ has done, and yet it's going to fall, too, because I'm going to put what Christ has done into motion in my life. This giant must go down and will go down and has gone down. It must stop talking to me, because God wants me to live free. God wants to get the glory of being the Liberator of my life. This giant isn't going to harass me anymore. God is going to be seen as the champion of my life. That's why Goliath *must* fall."

Yes, we do have a responsibility in this process. We need to lean together toward Jesus in faith and action. It's not a mild action we're taking. It's grace-filled, strong, and even severe. If there's any voice in your head that says, *Nope. Your giant will taunt you forever. You're not going to do it. You'll always need to live with things the way they are. Life will never change for the better*, then I want you to know that voice isn't the voice of Jesus. And that voice can—and will—be silenced!

Jesus came to this earth to complete a beautiful work. He took hell for us on the cross so that our relationship with God could be restored. Jesus rose from the grave so we could shake off the prospect of a doomed life and walk in that same power that brought him to life again.

You don't need to live with a taunting, debilitating giant any longer. Your giant is going down. In fact, your giant *must* go down. Jesus will do it for you, and in the pages ahead, I'll show you how that happens.

Your invitation is to lean into the work of Christ and to activate all that he has won for you.

You are closer than you think to a life that's not diminished any longer. A life of true freedom. A life that fully radiates God's glory.

—Louie Giglio

CHAPTER 1

Bigger Than Your Giant

—

Recently a woman was mauled to death by her *pet* tiger.

I was saddened by this tragic event. But I also thought what most sane people must have thought when they read the story: *Why would anyone have a pet tiger?* (No offense if you've got a pet Bengal in your backyard.)

Tigers are meat eaters! They survive in the wild by hunting and killing their prey. And a tiger will always be a tiger. So why would anyone try to tempt nature by making a pet out of one of these natural-born killers?

Here's what I think happened. When the woman first met the tiger, it looked cute and cuddly. That furry little cub was small and playful. Entertaining. Endearing. I bet she held that cub tight and it purred with delight. A bond was formed. She gave her pet tiger cub a name. Maybe Mooshie or BooBoo or Stripey or Elwood. She took it home with her and gave it a warm space to sleep and a safe place to play. All was well, day after day after day after day.

Until.

Elwood.

Grew.

Then that playful pet morphed into what it truly was and showed its true colors. It wasn't a fuzzy cub anymore. It was a savage killer. The tiger attacked and the results were heartbreaking.

It's not much different with our giants—the habits, the behaviors, the faulty beliefs, the same old broken ways we're accommodating in our lives.

These "pets" started out as cute and cuddly babies. They didn't look like they'd do us any harm. They were comforting. Reassuring. We formed bonds with these pets, and gave them a warm place to stay in our minds and hearts and behaviors.

But these same pets have grown. They're showing their true colors—and they aren't pets anymore. They're savage killers. Nine-foot-tall giants. They're ripping into us, mauling us.

We desperately want to rid ourselves of these giants.

But how?

My Own Pet Giant

———

Goliath wasn't born nine feet tall. And whatever has a stranglehold on you most likely didn't arrive on day one with threats of clenching you between its teeth. I'm guessing it was comforting and spoke to a need you had buried within. Your *killer* was camouflaged as a friend you couldn't live without. But, on the day not of your choosing, the gloves came off and the giant stepped on your throat, suffocating you with all its weight.

I've chronicled such a giant in my life in other talks and writings, and been up front about the tipping point where I fell into a deep, dark hole of depression and anxiety. If one of these behemoths is making life unbearable for you, I get it. For a time it was identified as my "anxiety disorder," a nice generic term generally accepted by people. Yet, over time, I have been able to more acutely pinpoint the giants that shoved me over the edge and into that pit. For me, understanding that anxiety is not *a thing*, but a symptom of *something(s)*, has been a game changer in dealing with the enemies of God's glory in my life.

To put it mildly, I had a breakdown. That was pretty obvious to everyone around me, and a nonnegotiable reality for me. The day arrived when the baby tiger was grown. It took aim, and the consequences were drastic and almost deadly. But what's more helpful is to understand *why*. I've come to learn it's usually not the result of one thing or one moment, but a combination of lots of things that fester over time, rotting us from the inside until we come unhinged.

So what pushed me into the hole of anxiety and depression? Genetic tendencies? No doubt. The rush and crush of having the engine revved too high for too long? For sure. Worry? Check.

But looking back I see the footprints of two of my own Goliaths: control and approval. I have a tendency to want to change whatever environment I am in. I want to make things better. I see what is, but I dream of what can be. I think like this driving through a city, sitting in traffic, eating in a restaurant, walking through a slum in Haiti, passing time between flights in an airport, waiting in a hospital. Anywhere. Anytime. I am thinking of how to create change, cast vision, and marshal people toward a common goal.

Being a change leader can be good. But it can also invite the baby cub of control into the mix. Some of you know what I mean. You're trying to control every outcome for your kids. You're sweating the stock market. You monitor all the conversations that flow throughout your crew, wanting to make sure everyone thinks the right thing and comes to the right conclusions. And like me, you find yourself staring at the ceiling when you should be deep in sleep, wondering which approach will work best to bring about the conclusion you are convinced is right.

Wanting to steer toward great outcomes is noble. But trying to control the world is disastrous. In time, controllers crack under the reality that none of us are in control.

Then there's the giant of approval. Couple my need to control with my underlying need to be liked and you have a perfect storm. This was especially true in the early days of planting the church we shepherd. Before we planted Passion City Church, being a speaker and ministry entrepreneur had been challenging for sure. We crafted stadium events in countries around the globe and forged a record label to bring music to the worldwide church. I spoke here, there, and everywhere. But if people didn't like me there was always another opportunity around the corner. Another conference. Another group of people. Another endeavor to launch.

But in planting a church you sink roots with a tribe, and in leading people week by week you quickly discover you can't please everyone. Sadly, I thought I could make everyone happy (*control* is talking now). And I really needed to, more than I wanted to admit. In our embryonic days, my wife, Shelley, and I got an e-mail from a friend that shattered any notion that planting a church would be easy, or that our good intentions would always be rewarded. When the giant of control met and married the giant of rejection, they tag-teamed me, tied my hands, and hurled me over the cliff. It wasn't anyone's fault but mine. Character flaws that were once smaller and manageable were now towering over me. Taunting me. Defying my God.

I was a controller who'd found he couldn't control anymore. I was an approval-seeker who'd discovered not everything he did was applauded. My pet tiger cub was a full-grown adversary I had to admit and deal with.

These are (I initially wrote *were*, but that's not as realistic as I'd like it to be) a couple of my giants.

What about you?

When One Voice Shuts You Down

———

For some of you, as soon as you read the title of this book, you knew exactly what your giant was. You didn't even need to think about it, because you battle against it every day.

Others aren't exactly sure what the name of their problem is because it's not as clear. All they know is something isn't right and they want to fix it.

A few, who read early copies of the manuscript, noted they didn't think they had any giants until they read a little more.

Either way, it's helpful to articulate what kind of giants can do us the most harm.

- Maybe a giant called fear rules our lives. It's not like we walk around shaking in our boots all the time. But in our most honest moments, we know anxiety is a big piece of who we are. It shakes us up and rattles our world. It makes us dread the nighttime. The fear has begun to dominate us, and at the end of the day we know it diminishes God's glory in our life.

- Maybe we're battling rejection. We grew up in a performance-based environment, and because of that we're afraid that if we don't get everything perfect we're not going to get the approval we long for. We fear that people will only love us if we produce the needed result. If we ever

take a break, if we ever turn in something less than perfect, if we ever say the wrong thing, if we ever show up in
the wrong outfit, if we ever go slower than the frantic pace
we're going now, then all that approval is out the window.

- Maybe a giant called comfort has taken hold. Comfort isn't
wrong if we're talking about genuine rest that refreshes us.
But comfort can become a huge problem if it morphs into
complacency or entitlement. Too often we embrace the
easiest path, the bare minimum, the "cush" job, the spoils
of this life. But the easiest path might not be the best path,
the path that Jesus invites us to take.

- Maybe the giant that harms us is anger. Not rage, neces-
sarily. Yet something smolders inside. We can't keep a lid
on our temper. Every once in a while we lash out for no
good reason. Something jumps out of us in anger, and we
wish we could take it back. We know this anger is shut-
ting down God's best for us, but we just can't seem to get
a handle on it.

- Maybe we are flat-out stuck in an addiction. Lots of different addictions taunt us, and most of us struggle with at
least one. The addiction might be to a substance or behavior that's controlling us—alcohol, drugs, porn, gambling,
shopping, or binge eating. Or maybe the addiction is to
something subtle. The wrong kind of friend. A wrong kind
of thought. Maybe we always feel we need to be the care-
taker of other people—doing for them what they should

do for themselves. Or we feel victimized if people don't give us the respect or love we think we deserve. Maybe we're always defensive. Or critical. We manipulate people. Or blame them. Our feelings have a way of hurting the relationships that matter, and we're not sure what to do. *Well, this is just the way I am,* we tell ourselves—and some days we even believe that lie.

Maybe we find ourselves tolerating the harmful thing at first, even though we know it clearly goes against God's plan. Maybe we try to justify its existence. We wrestle with it and wish it were gone. We're annoyed the harmful thing is there in the first place, but we end up giving it free rent anyway. Before we know it, the harmful thing has established a foothold. It becomes a giant. A default routine is formed. Our giant becomes a habit in the way we think or act. Some days we fight to rid ourselves of the giant, but the problem never seems to go away entirely.

How do we get rid of the giants? Jesus offers an abundant life to everyone who follows him. "The thief comes only to steal and kill and destroy," Jesus said; "I have come that they may have life, and have it to the full" (John 10:10). Jesus didn't come to earth to die on the cross and be resurrected from the grave so we could settle for a reduced amount of God's best. Jesus intended for us to "really live" (1 Thessalonians 3:8). And that means we can live freely in the power of what he has accomplished for us.

It starts with seeing and believing that whatever giant we're battling might be big—but it's *not* bigger than Jesus. Nine feet tall is nothing to him. And he intends to set you free.

We're going to see this in a powerful way as we unpack the story of David and Goliath. I'm guessing you've heard this tale somewhere along the line. If not, get ready. It's a gripping tale jammed with possibility for you. I've heard this story since my days as a kid in church. But there's a fresh twist that's been exploding in my heart more recently. A life-altering way of seeing Jesus in the story that changes everything about the way your giant is going down.

The Kid Comes to Death Valley

The backdrop of the story of David and Goliath, to catch us all up to speed, is that the ancient army of the Philistines was fighting against the army of Israel, the people of God. This was a pattern all throughout the Old Testament: the Philistine army was a constant thorn in the side of God's people, and the two armies often clashed. The Philistines have a god of their own, an idol we'll see more about in a moment. They were vile and surly, haters of the people who claimed allegiance to the one true God.

A lot of times throughout the story of Scripture, the Philistines had the upper hand, and that was the case when this particular story unfolds in 1 Samuel 17. Here's the backdrop.

Picture a particular valley in ancient Israel. It's stubbly and rocky and green and thorny. It's called the Valley of Elah, and through that valley flows the Brook of Elah. You'd think such a bucolic scene would be peaceful, inviting. But it isn't. It's soon going to be the valley of death.

Flanking each side of the brook is a hillside. The Philistine army was camped on one hillside, and the army of Israel was camped on the other side. Each army would camp in their tents at night, then each morning they'd come out to their places of battle. They could look right across the valley to stare each other down.

When our story opens, the two armies weren't doing much actual fighting. The army of Israel was being held back from advancing—and the guy holding back the Israelites from doing their real work was a crude brawler named Goliath, a big, huge, giant Philistine, nine feet tall, a champion fighter, a fierce and awesome-looking black-bearded warrior with thick body armor.

Every day Goliath would come out and yell insults at the army of Israel. He'd stride right down into the valley with his army behind him, glare up at the opposing hillside at the Israelite army, and shout with a sneer, "Cowards! You and your God are not big enough to take on us. I challenge you to a fight, and I defy your God! If anyone's brave enough to fight me, then come on down. Whoever wins the fight will win the whole war. The losing army will serve the winning army. All you gotta do is get past me." (That's not exactly what it says in 1 Samuel, but you get the idea.)

Day after day Goliath did this. A week passed. Two weeks. Three weeks. Four. Day after day, the insults continued. Day after day, none of the Israelites dared to go down to fight. The Bible says Goliath did this for a full forty days, yet even then, not a single soldier from the highly trained army of the people of God could stomach the thought of facing Goliath alone. Goliath must have let out a slew of insults. He shouted and taunted. He harassed and mocked. He agitated and coaxed and cajoled and scoffed, but still no one would fight him alone.

The Israelite army was intimidated.

Demoralized.

Immobilized.

Sunk.

The sound of a single bad voice had shut down the Israelites. Can you relate? They'd lost the fight, and they hadn't even gone to battle yet.

Step back for a moment and consider who the ancient Israelites were. It's hard to know exactly why they'd allowed themselves to become so intimidated. God had a rich history with these people. He'd chosen them as his own. He'd given them his presence. All they had to do was look to their times gone by to see how God had miraculously removed them from slavery in Egypt. He'd spilt the sea wide-open before them. Once they were safely through, its waters crashed down and wiped out the enemies pursuing them. He'd guided them through the Sinai wilderness with a cloud in the day and by fire at night. When they were thirsty, God made water appear. When they were hungry, God gave them manna to eat. He'd taken them across the Jordan River and brought them into the promised land. They'd conquered the highly fortified city of Jericho thanks to God's mighty outstretched arm. A shout of praise brought Jericho's walls tumbling down. Time and time again, God had done miraculous things for his people.

But they'd forgotten.

They weren't tapping into how all-powerful their God was, and how if they would just trust him and follow him and lean into him, then they'd have access to that same power in their lives again.

In fairness, we've got to give the Israelite army a bit of a break. Personally, I've never fought a nine-foot giant before. I've never really fought another human being before, and I can't say that I'd have the grit to go up against an armor-plated warrior standing three feet taller than me.

But what if he had threatened the people I love? There's a good chance I'd take a shot at a nine-foot giant then. Particularly if I had a sword in my hand and my own armor on. Yet not a single one of the Israelites were willing to enter into the fray. Every day the people of God were shut down by one harassing voice. What a gloomy thought. One loud, uncouth man was paralyzing the entire army of God.

Fortunately, help was on the way. And it was coming from an unlikely source.

On the fortieth day, a kid named David came up to the

outskirts of the Israelite camp. Most folks at the time didn't think David was anything special. The only person who'd ever thought much of him was an old prophet named Samuel, who'd come to the family's house once and anointed David's head with oil. But that had been awhile back. David was the youngest of a whole raft of older brothers. They were taller than he was. Tougher than he was. More handsome.

While the men in the family went off to do the fighting, David's job was to stay home with his aged father and take care of the family sheep.

On that particular day when he came to camp, David was bringing supplies to his older brothers who were up on the line. Basically, David was just a delivery boy.

The kid everybody yelled at to bring more cheese.

Remember the Training

———

Just at the very moment David was saying hello to his brothers, Goliath emerged on the other hill and started yelling his daily insults at the army of God. And in that moment, something snapped inside David. I picture him doing a double take. He was like, "Wait a minute . . . What's this overgrown ape yelling at us?"

The voice of Goliath came clearer, and the giant yelled, "You idiots are actually putting your trust in the God of Israel? Your

God is worthless. He's weak. He's nothing—just like you're nothing. Our god can smash your God."

David's eyes narrowed. His lips tightened. Incredulous, he asked his brothers, "Who is this joker? How is he getting away with saying all this about our God? Why is nobody taking him on? Why is nobody fighting?!"

David's brothers stammered, "Yeah, well, take a good look at this guy. His name is Goliath, and he comes out every day and does this. Nobody wants to fight him. It's a suicide mission, kid. Certain death. Just shut up and bring me another hunk of bread."

David glared across the valley.

"I'll fight him," he quipped. "I'm going to shut him up."

What?

Imagine how David's announcement went over with David's brothers.

I mean, picture a boxing match. Who would you pick?

In the red corner wearing nothing but sandals and a tunic is a runt of a kid named David. No armor. No sword. No shield. No army training.

And in the other corner, wearing a hundred and twenty-five pounds of steel-plated armor, is an experienced enemy warrior. He's head and shoulders taller than Shaquille O'Neal and ripped head to toe with solid muscle. Highly trained in all kinds of combat. Carries a spear. A sword. Huge helmet. Has an infinite supply of ammunition. He's got a separate armor bearer just to carry all his gear. He's got a full army at his back. Breathes fire. Crushes mere men.

Whatever giant we're battling might be big— but it's *not* bigger than Jesus.

Yeah, *that's* a fair fight.

David's brothers were like, "Kid, you're embarrassing us. The Israelite army is filled with experienced fighters, and none of them are willing to take on Goliath. Now you want to fight him? You've lost your mind. Get lost before we tell Dad."

But David hadn't lost his mind, because David has had some real-life training to fall back on. This wouldn't be his first fight. Earlier, in all those years when David had been out in the pasture tending sheep, he'd actually been receiving a very advanced education. His Trainer was none other than God himself, and little by little God was revealing his righteous and mighty character to David.

Part of David's training was writing songs about God, studying the facts and history of his people, and learning who God was and what God had done. Another part of David's training had been far less academic, far less poetic. Far more hands on.

One day a huge bear growled his way up to David's flock and grabbed one of the prized lambs. It was David's job to rescue the lamb. There was no one to call. No help in sight. So David went after the bear and rescued the sheep from its mouth. Ever see the movie *The Revenant*? Remember the scene when the bear mauled Leonardo DiCaprio? That's the kind of predator we're talking about. But when that bear turned on David, the shepherd boy seized it by its hair, struck it, and killed it.

This type of fight didn't happen only once. Another afternoon a huge roaring lion came up to the flock and had the same idea. David took his shepherd's rod and beat the lion lifeless. David had survived many harrowing, life-threatening battles. He knew these victories happened thanks to the power of God.

In the shadow of Goliath's taunts, David recounted these same stories of victory at the Israelites' camp. Those stories must have given him some credibility, because after David made his offer, word soon trickled up to King Saul, who had David brought to his tent. David told the stories to Saul and gave glory to God for the results. David said, "Your servant has killed both the lion and the bear; this uncircumcised Philistine will be like one of them, because he has defied the armies of the living God. The LORD who rescued me from the paw of the lion and the paw of the bear will rescue me from the hand of this Philistine" (1 Samuel 17:36–37).

Saul stood frozen for a moment.

"Okay. That's a pretty good résumé right there. You killed a bear? *And* a lion?"

The king scanned the boy's frame.

"Nobody else wants to fight him, but you can have a turn if you're so confident about it all. We're going to let you have a go at Goliath. But wait—at least put on some armor first. No? You don't have any armor. Here—wear mine."

David put on a couple pieces of the king's armor. It was shiny and solid, the best of the best. But David wasn't used to it and could hardly walk. "This isn't going to work for me," David said. "I need to take this off. God's got another plan."

David went down to the brook and selected five smooth stones from the edge of the water. He put the stones in his shepherd's bag, took out his sling, and went out to face the giant.

To cut to the chase, this one didn't last long. If you'd paid a lot of money for a ringside seat or a pay-per-view pass, you'd have been disappointed. But the action, though swift, was stunning.

Goliath and David exchanged a few key words. David took out one stone, slung it at the giant, and the giant fell at his feet, dead. *Bam.*

The fight was a first-round knockout. Ten seconds after the opening bell, everything was over except the popcorn and sweeping up.

One Giant, Two Giants, Three, a Dozen

Why is this story such a major backdrop for the Christian faith? Is it only so we can have a powerful youth camp message and an awesome animated talk for kids? Or is it because God wants us to all know it's possible for huge giants to go down cold?

You might have a nine-foot-tall behemoth in your life, one that taunts and intimidates you day after day after day. But with the power of God, that giant will fall. It doesn't matter the size of a problem. God's power and might are always greater.

Or it could be a whole string of giants you're battling. There may be problems and temptations coming at you from every side. The same was true in Scripture. Did you know Goliath isn't the only giant mentioned in the Bible? He was actually a descendent of a whole line of oversized nefarious warriors. Read 1 Chronicles 20, and the names of these other giants sound like the result of a laboratory potion gone wrong. There's Sibbekai and Sippai and Elhanan and Lahmi, and even a gargantuan fighter with six fingers on each hand and six toes on each foot.

God doesn't want us to be demoralized if we face more than one giant that needs to be taken down. He's able to take them all. And we'll soon see he already has.

If some form of bondage is in our lives, if some attitude seemingly can't be shaken, if some character flaw apparently can't be overcome, if some thought darkens our mind, if some problem has sunk its teeth into our life and we can't shake it as we move through our day, then take heart, because none of these giants are a match for Jesus. All these giants can—and will—fall.

Do we believe that?

Do we want to be free?

Jesus wants to assure us that he is completely and totally able to take down the giants in our lives. It may look as though the six-fingered, six-toed, furious, foaming, fearless thing coming at us can't be beaten. But through the power of Jesus, whatever needs to be overcome can—and will—come down.

The Ultra-Important
Twist to the Story

———

Over the next chapters, we're going to look at a variety of common, harmful giants—issues that look huge and unconquerable, ones a lot of people wrestle with. And we're going to see how these giants will fall. But you're not going to be left standing alone with a mantra of "you can do it if you try." You're going to meet a fighter who can do what you alone cannot do.

That's important, because this isn't any old self-help book we could pull off a bookstore shelf, skim through in ten minutes, and afterward have three shiny action plans that help us lead better, more prosperous lives. The big idea of this book isn't about us trying harder or rolling up our sleeves and working to improve our lives through our effort. The message of this book is that God extends his grace and favor toward us to allow us to experience his supernatural power. It's about us agreeing with him and letting his Holy Spirit work in our lives to put us on right paths, right ways of thinking and living.

That's where the big twist in this story comes in.

While I get that the story of David and Goliath is familiar to a lot of us, there is one important angle to this story that will help make it come alive in our hearts. Chances are, this shift sets this book apart from anything you've ever been taught before on David and Goliath. I'll discuss this twist in more depth in later chapters, but I want to present the idea here so we catch a glimpse of the freshness and relevance of this familiar story right up front. It's this:

We are *not* David in the story of David and Goliath.

Picture yourself at church or a conference. A speaker is going through the story of David and Goliath and he's really firing you up, saying something like this: "Come on, folks. David was a young person, and you're a young person too—or at least you're young at heart. David won the victory, so now you can win the victory too. David took up his sling. David selected his five smooth stones. David marched up on the battlefield. David took down the giant. If you want to take down your giant, then all you gotta be is just like David. Just get your sling. Select your stones. And aim big!"

Everybody gets a little amped at a message like that. We think, *Yeah. Okay. That's me. I can do this. I just need to have some more courage already. I just need to aim right. I can take down my giant with one shot, and I'm really gonna go big this time.*

What happens? Maybe we get extra brave for a little while. Maybe we double our efforts and tackle the problem of our giant with renewed enthusiasm. But this is only us trying to put on Saul's armor. It doesn't fit. At the end of the day or the conference or the next week, we go right back to living with our giant taunting us. The bumper sticker methodology that promises "You can do it" or "Dare to be a David" or "Become braver" just doesn't work in our lives, and our giant remains.

Here's why: we are *not* David in this story. That's a man-centered interpretation of the story of David and Goliath. You know who David is in our story?

Jesus.

Jesus is David in the story of David and Goliath. Jesus is the giant killer.

Does that fact not wake us all up? Hello? We are not David. You are not David. I am not David. Jesus is David! Jesus fights the battles for us. Jesus stares down the face of impossible odds. Jesus takes up his sling. Jesus selects five smooth stones. Jesus takes aim at the giant. The giant falls because of the work of Jesus.

We are called to participate with Jesus, sure. We are called to follow his leadership and align ourselves with the direction he's going. But mere human thinking or mere human power—if it's only human thinking or only human power—can never produce a supernatural result.

I know what you might be thinking: *Are you telling me we've had this story wrong the whole time? How is that possible?*

What I am helping us see is that while we can (and should) take courage from the shepherd boy and walk in greater confidence in life, the whole of Scripture points not to our abilities, but to Jesus as the Savior of the world. On every page, and in every story, Jesus can be seen—victorious, steadfast, able, trustworthy, mighty, loving, worthy.

As long as our eyes are on the problem, and the solution lies within ourselves, the X's are going to pile up on the calendars of our fight, marking the days little to nothing has changed. But all that changes the day Jesus enters our Valley of Elah. The moment we stop staring at our giant and lock eyes with Jesus. The moment our hope shifts from us to him.

In the story of David and Goliath, God did not want victory to come about because David was fitted out with all the best armor and held a sword in his hands and was really brave and defied the odds and had a whole army at his back.

God wanted victory to come simply because one young man trusted in him.

The Power of Seeing

All through this book, and throughout our fight, worship is going to be the soundtrack that leads us to victory. Ultimately, this is a book about worship.

If you're thinking, *Wait a minute, I need a book about fighting my bad habits and enemies . . . not a book about church songs and music,* don't freak out. Worship is simply a shift of attention that allows us to see God better. Worship is like corrective lenses for our souls, bringing God clearer into view. That's important for all of us, especially when life goes off the rails.

Worship puts God in focus. When the Almighty is in view, our giant's power over our thinking begins to flicker and fade.

Once the giants of control and approval had washed me down the tubes, I was a wreck physically and mentally. During the roughest stretch I was in a different doctor's office every week. I couldn't sleep through the night. Doctors helped me out of the dark pit. Praising God led me into the light. Real change began to creep into the equation when the roots of control and approval were dislodged and disrupted.

While change didn't happen in one fell swoop (I'm still growing and healing today), the difference came when I shifted my thinking before I closed my eyes at night. As I named the things that I sought to control, I would say to myself, *That belongs to God.* I would remind myself that if God wants a certain result, it would happen. If he didn't, why would I? I began lifting my eyes to the One who is *actually in control.* The result: my giants had to stop talking, or if they were still talking, I stopped listening.

I need someone bigger than my giant to set my gaze on. Otherwise, I listen needlessly to a dead Goliath when the Maker of heaven is holding me in his hands.

I don't know what's keeping you up at night or making you want to stay under the covers all day. But I do know Jesus is on your side. He is fighting for you and he has won. That's not hype.

Nor empty rhetoric. Jesus has, in fact, defeated every foe. And he is inviting you to come and see what he has done.

That's what I love about the next few pages we are about to journey through. Together, we will see that Jesus is far more than just a good idea. He is the all-sufficient source for all we need, available every step of the journey and in every hour of our battle.

But it's still a fight, because even dead giants can still call your name.

CHAPTER 2

Dead but Still Deadly

During summers as a kid, I used to go to youth camp with my church. We went to Hilton Head Island, South Carolina, but not to stay in some fancy condominium by the ocean. We stayed at the Presbyterian campground, situated on a track of land on the other side of the main road from the ocean in an area that could most appropriately be called "jungle-esque."

When I say "jungle-esque," I mean the campground was definitely a wild land overgrown with swampy forests. This was the 1970s, long before most of the modern developments on Hilton Head Island had been built. The island itself is maybe sixty square miles. To reach the camp, we turned off the main road into a smaller driveway that led us inside the grounds. The campground was comprised of a dining hall and kitchen (with the expected tetherball pole out front and a four-square court lined on the entryway floor) and a rustic chapel that seated about one hundred people. There were five girls' cabins and five guys' cabins located on opposite sides of the softball field. A long one-lane sandy trail led from the main area to the cabins. It was fine during the day, but we wouldn't walk it at night without a flashlight. In the middle of each cabin cluster was a bathhouse, and bathhouses didn't have doors or windows. The bathhouses were completely vulnerable to the elements.

That's where the fun started.

At night, if you needed to go to the bathroom, you had to traipse outside your cabin and scamper down the path to reach the bathhouse. You never knew what sort of wildlife might be lurking on the way. Lizards ran the place. Spiders were ever-present.

And then there were snakes.

Lots of snakes. Poisonous snakes. You'd hope you didn't encounter one on the way to the bathhouse at night, or worse, one would already be in the stall!

At the start of each week, a handful of skittish kids would take one glance at those bathrooms and make the dubious decision *not* to make that journey at night, no matter what the cost.

Predators aside, I loved it on Hilton Head. And I loved that Presbyterian camp. So many special steps of my early walk with Jesus trace back to that place. The first week was solely for six and seventh graders. Then came a weekend break. Then another week for eighth and ninth graders. Another weekend break. Then a final week for eleventh and twelfth graders. If you were a college student you could be a counselor, which meant you could come the weekend before the first week of camp started and help set up, then stay for the off weekend and repeat. If you timed it right, you could spend a month on Hilton Head Island.

One of the jobs for counselors during the off weeks was to spread lime around each of the cabin areas. Snakes apparently hate lime. We wanted to let these snakes know we were here, and they didn't want to mess with us. Hey—they could have their territory. We could have ours. If all went well, they'd get the idea we were here to stay for a while. They'd go back to wherever they came from and everything would be peaceful.

Sometimes the lime proved an effective blocker, and sometimes it didn't. When campers started spotting too many snakes on the bathroom trail, that meant we counselors needed to up the ante. On weekends when campers were gone, my best friend Andy Stanley and I took matters into our own hands. We used the "we just want the girls to feel safe" excuse to go out hunting with another buddy or two. We wanted to let the snakes know we weren't kidding around. These were poisonous snakes, keep in mind, fully capable of seriously hurting us.

Our hunts went like this. Once it got dark (snakes like to move when the weather cools), we'd head out into the overgrown areas between the cabins with a flashlight in one hand and a baseball bat in the other. We spread out about ten to fifteen feet from one another and slowly moved through the ankle-high growth. It never took too long before we'd find our prey.

Bingo—a three-foot-long copperhead would cruise through the grass in front of us.

Our technique of doing away with snakes wasn't über-sophisticated. This was absolutely low-level combat. We were teens and didn't really think this plan through. For crying out loud, we had on shorts and tennis shoes. No steel-toe boots. No leg protectors. Nope.

Once we spotted a prey, we'd glance around to make sure the copperhead's brother wasn't right behind him. Then we'd take our baseball bat and smack the snake on the head. *Bam!* Then we'd hit it fifty more times on the head just to make sure the job was done right. *Bam! Bam! Bam! Bam! Bam!* (It's amazing how focused your aim can be when a snake bite is likely if you miss!)

Once that snake was good and dead, we'd press the end of the barrel down on what was left of the snake's head. Next we would grab the snake's body and yank hard. The snake's head would snap right off, and we'd grind it further down into the sandy soil and bury it with more sand.

Isn't that lovely?

Now what to do? You can't exactly leave the rest of the snake lying in the grass. That would cause one of the other guys to panic in a later moment, not knowing the snake was finished. So, we'd swallow hard and pick the headless snake up by the tail. Then we'd go on to look for the next snake. After an hour we'd each have a dozen dead snakes in one hand while we tried to juggle the flashlight and baseball bat with the other.

A funny thing about dead snakes: the head might be gone, but the snake's body will continue to squirm a long time afterward. So we'd be walking around in the woods at night with a mess of dead snake bodies crawling up our arms. We all tried to be cool, but it personally gave me the willies. I'd remind myself the snakes weren't actually alive. *Yep, I bonked that snake on the head. I ground its head into the dirt. I yanked the head off and buried it. The snake is dead, Louie; the snake is definitely dead.*

But then another body would wrap itself on my arm.

When our snake-hunting expedition was over, we'd walk to the center of camp where the dining room and chapel were. We'd pile up the bodies, and they'd keep writhing in a little headless pile for a while. I don't remember what we did with them after that. Probably some sort of teen shenanigans. So why do I tell this story? Why am I creeping you out with tales of writhing? There's an important purpose to telling it today, I promise. The danger of dead snakes can actually help us picture some critical truths related to taking down our giants.

A Crushed Snake. An Alive Jesus.

―――――

When a dead snake's body squirms, it might make the hair on your neck stand up, but that's all it can do: give you a little scare. Make your blood pressure spike.

A dead snake's head, however, can still be extremely dangerous. Back on Hilton Head, we buried the heads of those dead snakes. Why? Because there's still enough venom in the fangs to do serious damage to a person. If you're out walking around in the woods and step on a dead snake's head, then it's likely enough poison is spring-loaded in a fang where any pressure can release the poison into your foot. That's big trouble.

The danger of dead snakes doesn't provide an exact analogy, of course, but they picture much of the God-truth we're trying to unfold in this book. Satan was defeated on the cross. The battle was over. The victory was won. That's all past tense. Thanks to the death, burial, and resurrection of Jesus, Christ has rendered Satan powerless. But Satan can still wriggle and squirm and make the hairs on our necks stand up. If we step on Satan's fangs, he can still poison us and cause serious harm. We're not in heaven yet, and the Enemy is still prowling around on planet Earth. His body is still flailing about, and he is still dangerous. If we listen to the Enemy, or if we follow his evil schemes, or if we mess with any of the practices he lays claim to, we will self-inject that poison into our lives. The poison will diminish our hope and weaken the abundant reality of what our lives can be in Christ.

So there are two truths to keep in mind. One: Satan was defeated on the cross. Jesus has won the victory. End of story. And two: the snake still wriggles. The snake still has venom. It's a now-and-not-yet reality. Catch the paradox? These two truths

Your giant is *dead*. And yet . . . your giant is still *deadly*.

seem contradictory, but they're not. When it comes to your giant going down, both of these truths are equally true.

Your giant is dead.

And yet . . .

Your giant is still deadly.

Maybe your first response is that you don't believe this is true. You're thinking, *Louie, wait a minute. There's no way my giant is dead. He's every bit alive. In fact, my giant was demoralizing me this very morning. My giant taunts God all the time in my life. I've actually been under this giant's control this very night. This giant definitely has a hold on me.*

I get that feeling. You're grappling with the two overlapping realities. This calls for truth immersion. When we struggle with our giants, we sometimes mistakenly wish for Jesus to go to the cross all over again. We come to Jesus in prayer and say, "Jesus, I've got a giant. Please do something about it right now! Please do something big!" and we want something huge and supernatural and miraculous and brand new to happen.

But that's crazy, because what we're really expecting Jesus to say is this: "Fine. I'll go be whipped and scourged and mocked again for your giant. I'll travel down that narrow Jerusalem street, carrying a heavy Roman cross for the second time. I'll have the heavy spikes driven into in my hands and feet again. I'll take hell upon the cross again and cry out again, 'My God, My God, why have you forsaken me,' and I'll have my side pierced with a spear again—all for your giant. My body will be wrapped with heavy embalming cloths, and I'll be laid out in a borrowed tomb again. I'll be raised up on the third day again to give you victory over your giant."

That's not how it works. Paul says in Romans 6:9, "For we know that since Christ was raised from the dead, he cannot die again; death no longer has mastery over him." Jesus can't die again! That's actually a very good thing, and we need to immerse ourselves in that awesome reality. Jesus died one time—for all time. Jesus never needs to go to another cross. Period. The work of defeating death and all hell's power is finished. Completed. Done. Accomplished. Jesus has defeated all of sin, all of death, all of hell, all of darkness. Our giants have fallen. Goliath is dead from the hit to the head. He's sprawled out flat on the ground. Smashed nose. Dirt in eyes. Bugs in mouth. Hey, alert the vultures: there's good eating tonight.

We see this work of Jesus on the cross prophesied about way back in Genesis 3:15. Soon after the forbidden fruit was eaten in the garden of Eden by Adam and Eve, God cursed the tempter, the serpent, an embodiment of Satan. As part of this curse, God declared that Eve's offspring would one day ultimately crush the serpent's head. That offspring is Jesus. Jesus is the ultimate snake-crusher. Jesus demolished the snake, the Devil, with a defining and deafening blow. Death doesn't carry a sting anymore. Death was swallowed up in victory. Jesus Christ won the battle.

We see direct evidence of this In 1 John 3:8: "The reason

the Son of God appeared was to destroy the devil's work." That means that Jesus is not some puny god. He's not flimsy or frail or helpless or toothless. He has been given all authority (Matthew 28:18). And *all* means *all*. The reason Jesus came to earth was to crush the power of sin and death. That's what Jesus did. The work is finished. Another passage that speaks strongly to this is Hebrews 2:14–15: "Since the children have flesh and blood, he too shared in their humanity so that by his death he might break the power of him who holds the power of death—that is, the devil—and free those who all their lives were held in slavery by their fear of death."

Satan's power was broken on the cross. Yet even though Jesus completed the work on the cross, this is where we feel the paradox: Satan can still harm us. If you step on his fangs, you're going to feel the sting of his poisonous words and ways. That's a big part of the tension of living as a follower of Jesus today. We live in the great expanse of time and space between two awesome points: the cross and the final work of Jesus in the end times when everything is made right. In this space that we live in today, Satan has been defeated, yet he is still dangerous. First Peter 5:8 describes it this way: "Be alert and of sober mind. Your enemy the devil prowls around like a roaring lion looking for someone to devour."

I encounter so many people who love Jesus, sure. They believe in him. They want to follow him with everything they've got. They praise God. They want to live for him. Yet they're still accommodating some sort of debilitating giant in their lives. That giant is tormenting them, and it's taunting God. The evil power that fueled that giant is long crushed. But they didn't know to watch out for buried snake heads. They went walking in the woods at night, and the fangs shot venom into their feet.

The good news is that as followers of Christ we are not left defenseless. A way forward is made available in Scripture. James 4:7 tells us to "submit yourselves, then, to God. Resist the devil, and he will flee from you." Resisting means we make a stand against temptation. We choose the pathway of Jesus. With the power of God in our lives, we deliberately decide to draw close to him.

In simpler terms, don't step on the dead snake head.

Ephesians 6:10–18 further instructs us to "put on the full armor of God." Our armor is made of truth. Jesus has given us his righteousness. We have the gospel of peace in place. We have the shield of faith. We have the helmet of salvation and the sword of the Spirit, the Word of God.

Our armor isn't the old clunky armor of King Saul. That armor is man-made and only slows us down. We weren't designed to walk around in man-made armor and still be effective giant slayers. Our armor is God-made. It was forged in the fires of his holiness. It was handed to us by the power of his Spirit. It's available for us to wear anytime we wish. All that's required of us is to put it on.

The Unsearchable Riches of Christ

———

Our ultimate defense against giants—the best defense we have—is to lean into the all-sufficiency of Jesus. Maybe that's a term you've heard before—*all-sufficiency*—but you aren't quite sure what it means. Or maybe the term is brand-new to you. We need to unpack some scripture around this great truth: that Jesus is all-sufficient.

By *sufficient* we mean that Jesus is *enough*. He is all we need to fulfill God's greatest purposes for our lives. Jesus is not deficient in anything. Jesus is not lacking or inadequate or meager or poor. He's fully competent. He's fully abounding. Thanks to Jesus, we sit at a banqueting table every day; our cups are constantly overflowing, and our plates are constantly full.

In the last chapter we talked about how one of the big twists to applying the story of David and Goliath is to think of David as Jesus, not of us as David. Jesus is the one who fights the battles for us. Yes, we do have some responsibility. We submit to Jesus' plan. We resist the Devil using Jesus' power within us. We align ourselves with the person and work of Jesus Christ. Yet it's always Jesus who brings the giant down. Not us. That's part of what the term *all-sufficiency* is referring to.

One big problem we often have as followers of Jesus is that we want to function as if life all depends on us. We do this because that's what we're used to. Sure, we believe in God, and we believe Jesus saves. We believe that Jesus transforms our lives (Romans 12:2). We give lip service to the gospel, and we believe that it's all about grace. But if we have an addiction, or if we're troubled by fear or anger, or if we're caught in the sticky spider's web of needing the approval of man and want to get out, or if we're struggling to bring down some sort of other giant in our lives, then we're far too prone to want to do the work ourselves. We mistakenly believe it's all up to us to conquer the giant. We still function as if killing the giant depends upon us.

Lauren Chandler (wife of Matt Chandler, lead pastor of The Village Church in Dallas, Texas) articulates well this tendency. I'd say a lot of Jesus followers feel this way. She wrote,

> Three years into Matt's position as pastor of The Village Church, I entered a 12-step program. Let me quell the questions: I didn't "work the steps" because he became a pastor. I needed to recover from the addiction of being a good girl and performing my way into God's good graces. I said with my lips that salvation is by grace alone through faith alone. I even thought I believed this. But in my heart of hearts, I functioned as if it all depended on me. With my life I said, "God, thanks for saving me, but I've got it from here."
>
> So one Thursday night at the church, in front of those who only knew me as their pastor's wife, I stood up to say, "There's something the Lord is asking me to surrender." The

weight of what people would think of me nearly glued me to my seat and kept me from standing. But I felt something incredible the moment I rose to my feet. I felt weightlessness. I felt relief. And there were tears—lots and lots of tears. In all my anxiety over what the people would think of me— the gasps and whispers I thought I'd hear—I instead found fellowship. I wasn't untouchable or un-relatable. I became real to them—in real need of a real Savior.[1]

That's it! We're all in need of a real Savior—even Christians. We say with our lips that our salvation is by grace alone through faith alone. We believe that Jesus sanctifies us and transforms our lives by his power. But just like Lauren wrote, we make the mistake of trying to function as if it all depends on us. We say, "God, thanks for saving me. God, thanks for sanctifying me. But I'm good. I've got it from here. Thanks anyway, God. I can do this on my own."

If we truly want to change, then we need to understand our dependency on the all-sufficiency of Jesus Christ. Our change is more about trusting and less about trying. We've got to make this paradigm shift in our minds. Christ always does the real work. Christ is the real force for us to change.

Just imagine if Bill Gates walked up to you one day and handed you a check for a billion dollars. You could do a ton of noble things with that amount of money. Not to mention buy a condo tower for you, your family, and your friends to live in.

But what if you just let that check ride around in your pocket for the rest of your years? Would you still have the benefit of that gift? Theoretically, you'd be rich. But practically, you'd be a billion dollars poorer. When we follow Jesus, he hands us unlimited riches, but we need to cash the check too. Here's what that "check" looks like in Scripture; it's leaning into this truth: "His divine power has given us everything we need for a godly life through our knowledge of him who called us by his own glory and goodness" (2 Peter 1:3).

Read the first bit of that verse again if you need to. God's "divine power has given us everything we need for a godly life."

Stop right there. Focus on these three words . . .

"Everything we need."

That's our check. Unlimited riches. That's what we've been given in Christ. God has given us everything we need for our spiritual life. All joy. All value. All purpose. All hope. All comfort. All power to resist temptation. All power to change. All ability to live lives of godliness. All guidance and marked pathways to live for him.

Our task is to cash the check. It's to depend on Christ. Sure, that's not always easy to grasp. Particularly in the Western world where we like to be so self-sufficient. From an early age, we are taught to be proud, strong, and independent. None of those things are wrong, but when it comes to our Christian life, the paradigm has to shift. Jesus invites us to rest, to trust, to depend on him.

In the first three chapters of Ephesians, Paul notes the challenges of describing and grasping this wonder. It isn't easy. At last, Paul simply calls the riches "unsearchable" (Ephesians 3:8 NKJV). I love that word. *Unsearchable.* The unsearchable riches of Christ are like a huge cavern filled with gold that can never be fully explored. It's an incredibly complex math algorithm that solves all the problems of mankind. It can be tapped into, but it can never be fully understood or written in one sentence on a chalkboard. Christ's grace is readily available to us, yet in its entirety it's so amazing it's unfathomable.

My mentor back in those Hilton Head days, Dan DeHaan, talked about man's quest to grasp a full understanding of God's character being like a boy following a trickling brook as it flowed downstream. Step by step, as he followed each babble and turn, he learned more and more about the little brook. Soon, the brook he knew well widened into a fast-moving creek with deepening pools, and eventually flowed into a mighty river. As he walked the bank he grew to know the river well. Day by day he understood it better. Until one day he looked up and the river became an ocean.

Like our pursuit of the unsearchable riches of Christ, the more you get to know, the more you learn there's so much more to get to know.

Famed pastor and educator A. T. Pierson (1837–1911)

lamented his own human inadequacies in communicating to his congregation the depth and levels of the "unsearchable riches of Christ:"

> "Unsearchable" literally means riches that can never be [fully] explored. You can form no estimate of them, and never get to the end of your investigation. There is a boundless continent, a world, a universe of riches that still lies before you, when you have carried your search to the limits of possibility.
>
> I sink back exhausted, in the vain attempt to set before [my] congregation the greatest mystery of grace that I ever grappled with. I cannot remember, in thirty years of Gospel preaching, ever to have been confronted with a theme that more baffled every outreach of thought and every possibility of utterance than the theme that I have now attempted in the name of God to present.[2]

That's how huge the riches of Christ are. In Philippians 4:13, Paul talks about how we "can do all things through Christ who strengthens [us]" (NKJV). That's the all-sufficiency of Christ in practice. That is the picture of a person exploring the unsearchable universe of Christ's riches. That person is swimming in the boundless ocean of Christ's love. Paul wasn't doing "all things" because of Christ-plus-something. It was Christ-plus-nothing.

The power to change was simply . . .

Christ.

A Gross, Bloody, Hacked-Off Head

So let's zoom in on two often missed lines in the biblical story of David and Goliath. The first verse is 1 Samuel 17:50: "So David triumphed over the Philistine with a sling and a stone; without a sword in his hand he struck down the Philistine and killed him."

What's the important truth to remember? David didn't have a sword when he killed Goliath. The wallop of the initial sling and stone was enough to kill the giant. Goliath was already dead when he hit the ground. Yet the story doesn't end there, as we see in the very next verse: "David ran and stood over him. He took hold of the Philistine's sword and drew it from the sheath. After he killed him, he cut off his head with the sword" (v. 51).

This is key. David killed Goliath with only a sling and a stone. That's all it took. But then David sprinted over to the dead giant lying on the ground, yanked Goliath's sword from its scabbard, and hacked off the giant's head. Why all the gore, David? Why didn't you just shout out to the Israelites, "Giant down! Goliath's dead. He's not breathing. He's finished."

David was driving home a point. He wanted to be emphatic. He wanted everybody to know without a shadow of a doubt that the giant was definitely dead. What a picture. I hope the weight of the sword lopped off the head in one fell swoop, but maybe it didn't. Maybe it took a few hacks for David to get the job done. Either way, David the shepherd boy eventually grabbed that hacked-off head and carried it around. It must have had a bunch of blood dripping out and gross sinews hanging off of it. He showed it both to his own army, the Israelites, and to the opposing army, the Philistines. Why? Two reasons.

First, David didn't want anyone in his own army to have any fear. David was saying to them, "This giant is dead, guys. He's definitely dead. The victory is ours. God gave us this victory, and it's a complete victory. Run forward with a shout! The giant's head is hacked off and in my hands. Here—I'll show you the head for yourselves."

Second, David wanted the enemy army, the Philistines, to know for certain that the victory wasn't theirs. "Hey, enemy army—take a good look. Here's your champion now. His hacked-off head is right here in my hands. Take a close look at Goliath's mouth. Just a few minutes ago this very same mouth was taunting my God. But I don't hear this mouth talking anymore. And why's that? Oh yeah, because he's DEAD! So you remember that, enemy. You still got anything to say now about our God, the God of Abraham and Isaac and Jacob? You got any more insults to hurl at the God who spoke the universe into being, the God who created everything, the God of angel armies? No, I didn't think so."

David also kept the head to show King Saul (1 Samuel 17:57). A grisly image, sure, but that's the way people fought back then. Can you imagine the scene? David rolls into the tent: "Greetings,

O King. Nice to see you again, sir. I guess you saw it go down out there today. Goliath is not with us anymore, sir. But check out what I got. Whoops, sorry about the blood on the rugs." And Saul's like, "Yup. That giant is definitely dead. I recognize that mouth. For forty days it taunted God and humiliated his people. But now that mouth is quiet."

The very thing that had terrorized King Saul had now been rendered silent. Saul had nothing more to fear.

For us, our response to the image of the severed head should be to praise God for what he has done. We can look at the head of the giant and realize once and for all that the giant doesn't hold any more power over us. We don't need to be afraid of that gross and gruesome hunk of bloody flesh. We can say with confidence, "Hey, this thing used to harass me. But—praise God—it's just a skull with some meat on it now. The giant doesn't harass me anymore!"

When it comes to you and your specific giant, here's a very practical application. Don't *conceal* the severed head. Rather, *confess* the severed head. Tell a small group of trusted friends about the severed head of your giant—the same severed enemy's head that Christ holds in his hands. Point to Christ as the victor. Let people know that Jesus has conquered what had once harassed you.

See, whenever a problem is concealed, it finds power in the darkness. But when a problem is confessed, it loses that power. Confession brings the light of Christ to shine upon that problem.

In most cases when we confess something, people aren't all that shocked either. Usually the reaction is like, "Yeah, I kinda knew anyway."

Here's another way we depend upon the power of the name of Jesus. We pick up the sword of the Spirit, the Word of God, and we read Scripture out loud and we memorize truths so the light of Jesus constantly shines in our minds and hearts. We don't need to rationalize with our giants. We aren't called to argue with them. Jesus invites us into the truth of the situation. That huge, ferocious giant might be coming at us with a sword, spear, and javelin, but Jesus is bigger than our giant.

Guess what? When we do that, we're not battling our giant in our own strength and ability anymore. We're not battling our giant with our own armor on. We're battling the giant in the name of the Lord God Almighty, in the name of the risen Lord Jesus Christ. We're going to keep saying the name of Jesus, and saying that name and saying that name, until we truly believe that Jesus is who he says he is.

The God who fells giants.

High and Lifted up

———

It was important to me for you to have a foundation of big God-ideas in this chapter before going on with the rest of the book. In the chapters ahead, we're going to get more specific about what kinds of giants commonly immobilize and defeat people. I don't think we're struggling with a hundred giants. I've got a feeling the five we're going to talk about are going to hit really close to home.

And we'll get to the practical specifics of how they're coming down.

Our strategy for dealing with these giants will depend heavily on the all-sufficiency of Christ, so it's important to really dig into the truth of this chapter. We're not going to confront these problems by "becoming a David" or rallying the troops or crying out, "Hey, get your slingshots out, people!" Instead, we're going to rally around the gospel. Jesus is fighting for us, and he has won the war, defeated the Enemy. Yes, we need to participate with Jesus, and we're going to participate with him by his power and for his glory. That's what Jesus did when he went to the cross. He died for our freedom, but he also died for God's fame.

That means Jesus wanted to put to shame all the counterfeits, all the posers in the world, all the false gods and false security systems in the world who say, "I can be your god. Come to me, and I'll make you feel better. Come to me, and let me run the show."

Today Jesus says to us, "No, we're going to finish off that thinking once and for all, and I am going to prove that I am the one true Messiah and that my Father is the one true God. He is just and the Justifier. He's the one who can save, the only one who can bring your heart to life again. My Father is the only deliverer, the only one who can bring salvation to his people. He's the only one who can break the chains. He's the only one who can open the doors. He's the only one who can shut down the lies. He is God, and there is no other. He is a God of grace, a God of kindness, a God of compassion, a God of love, a God who would sacrifice his own Son for you and me. He is the Lord, and there is no other God."

So what do you do if your Goliath starts talking to you anytime soon? You remind him that he's dead. You start with the Jesus-talk. You stop listening to what Goliath is saying, and you start listening to what God is saying. Maybe all you take is a tiny step at first, but it's a big step for you to say, "Right here, right now I believe in the power of the name of Jesus."

Change isn't the result of a formula. Change might not be immediate for you. Your giant might not disappear in an instant. But you have the name, and the power, and the authority of the blood of the risen Lord Jesus Christ. You have the power of the cross, the power of Jesus' resurrection. Your giant may be big, but it is not bigger than the name of Jesus.

When you believe that Jesus is bigger than whatever it is you're facing, something is going to shift in you. Do you truly believe that? I'm not trying to hype this up. It doesn't need to be, because there is nothing more important and extraordinary than the work Jesus did on the cross. All our man-made enthusiasm can't come close to matching the glory of the God-bought victory that is ours. The victory is already here. We just need to have the Spirit of God infuse us with the reality of that amazing truth. We just need to have the Spirit of God pull us up to that height. Victory starts with changing our minds and believing that Jesus fought once and for all, and our giant has fallen.

If we let him, that same Jesus leads us into victory. Praise God. Not only will Goliath fall. He *must* fall. He must fall so Jesus can be exalted in this world.

Now it's time for the giant of fear to hit the ground.

CHAPTER 3

Fear Must Fall

—

Airplanes are my second home. Travel is a necessary part of my calling. It's been that way for years. Home base is Hartsfield-Jackson Atlanta International Airport, literally the busiest airport in the *world*. Its maze of concourses and trains can intimidate the occasional flyer commuting through our city, yet I can navigate the place with my eyes closed. For that matter, I can get through most major airports in America in my sleep.

Yet I'm sensitive to those who travel less frequently and to those who battle the anxiety of being trapped inside a thin metal tube thirty-five thousand feet above the ground. I know for many, the struggle is real.

Take, for example, the nice woman in the seat behind me a few months ago.

If you've ever flown to New York City, you know the approach to LaGuardia can be, uh . . . *interesting*, both in good and bad ways. Good-interesting, because often you get a wide-eyed view of the city and of Lady Liberty off to the left. Or possibly a nice glimpse of the shore out the right-side windows. Bad-interesting, because parts of the runway extend over water, and landings can evoke tears and ulcers. Then there's the weather in New York. During winter months (or even on a foggy day), landings at LaGuardia can get tricky in a hurry. Recently a jet skidded on the icy runway and came to rest only after it careened over a fence and stopped with its body partially over the open water.

So, back to the story of the woman seated behind me. As we descended into New York City, the pilot came over the PA system, giving his normal spiel. "Hi, folks," he calmly offered. "This is the captain from the flight deck. We're on our initial approach into New York. Uh, they're showing low visibility and a temperature of thirty-six degrees. There might be a few bumps, so I'm going to ask you to go ahead and take your seats and make sure your seat belts are fastened. Looks like we should have you on the ground in about twenty-three minutes. Flight attendants, please prepare the cabin for landing."

I looked up from the journal I was scribbling in and glanced out the window. Our flight path really wasn't that bumpy (at least not yet), but outside there was nothing to see except a thick, foggy blanket between us and the ground. I stared into nothing for a minute, thinking the grayish cotton-candy sky might part and reveal the rooftops below. No dice.

"Honey, I can't see the ground," said the woman behind me to her seatmate. She sounded older, and the nervousness in her voice was palpable. It was clear she was scared.

I couldn't make out her seatmate's reply, but the woman spoke again. "How can we land if we can't see the ground?" Her tone was one of despair. Her voice quaked.

The plane kept dropping in altitude as we neared the airport. It felt like we were still a good ways from touchdown, probably thousands of feet in the air, but I didn't know for sure. What I did know was that we were bound to break through this layer of fog sometime soon. A commercial airplane can't be landed in zero visibility. Certainly not on a runway that protrudes like a yardstick into the bay. Clarity was coming. We only needed to wait. But clearly the woman behind me was not an experienced flier. She didn't know the clouds were going to part. I could almost feel her hand gripping the armrest as her voice peaked: "I still can't see anything! I can't see the ground!"

She was legitimately frightened, and I felt compassion for her. I wanted to assure her that we were not going to land without seeing the ground. In just a few seconds, or minutes, the city would appear beneath us, and all would be okay. But it's difficult to convey things like that in a plane. She didn't know me or know I was an experienced flier. I doubted if any amount of information conveyed by a stranger would overcome the fear that had a stranglehold on her.

Just that instant, the plane dipped through the final bit of fog. The rooftops of houses and businesses appeared.

She shrieked, "I see the ground! Oh, there it is. I can see it! I can see it, honey. It's right there!" I could hear the relief in her voice.

Within minutes, the plane touched the tarmac. The wheels screeched with a slight bounce before the plane rumbled down the pavement to a stop. I gave the woman a little silent cheer.

Here's the point of this story: fear grips us whenever we believe that apart from, or in spite of, our best efforts, something undesirable is going to happen and we can't stop it. Sometimes fear is irrational, and sometimes it's rational. But no matter what kind of fear it is, it always affects us.

Fear is a big deal in the story of us and God. In Scripture, the commandment repeated the most is the commandment to *fear not*. Someone added these up, and apparently there are 366 "fear nots" in the Bible—one "fear not" for every day of the year—including Leap Year. Plus, there are a lot of related directives such as "Do not be afraid," "Take courage," and "Take heart."

The command to "fear not" fills Scripture—and we've got to ask why this commandment is so widespread. The answer must be that a lot of us have a lot of fears. Fear is a giant. One of the most common giants that must fall. Fear can taunt us and harm us. Fear can get a foothold in our lives and begin to dominate us. Fear can demoralize us and ultimately diminish God's glory in our lives. It never diminishes God's glory within God himself, because God's intrinsic worth cannot be changed. But the way we reflect God's glory gets diminished. The way we show the world who God is and the way we show ourselves who God is—that's what is lessened.

Fear doesn't always look like fear. And this is where this giant gains a buy-in from huge amounts of people. Sometimes fear is flat-out terror. It's shake-in-your-boots fright. But at other times this giant exhibits itself less overtly. It shows up as anxiety or nervousness or worry or stress or dread or tension or stomach problems. Fear chews away at our lives and erodes our sense of confidence and well-being. It robs us of sleep and rest. Fear blinds us and steals our praise.

What do we do with these fears? By the grace of God, how does this giant fall?

Digging Away the Layers

Right up front, let's remind ourselves of this powerful truth: the giant of fear can taunt us, but it doesn't have the ultimate power. Jesus has the ultimate power. Fear may seek to obscure our view of God and crush our confidence. Fear may get a grip on our throats and try to choke the very breath out of us. Fear may yell insults and try to convince us that we're going to live with this giant the rest of our lives. But the giant of fear is already dead. It's done for. It was conquered by Jesus on the cross. In the name of Jesus, the giant of fear must fall.

What's our part in agreeing with God? We understand that

we must hear Jesus and we must see Jesus. We must keep the focus of our hearts on him. That's because hearing Jesus and seeing Jesus and focusing on Jesus builds up our faith, and faith is the antidote to fear. The opposite of fear is not being bold and courageous. The opposite of fear is faith. And faith begins by us saying, "I have confidence in God that he is bigger than this giant."

Developing faith isn't an overnight fix. It might have taken a long time for us to fall into the hole of fearfulness, so it can take awhile to get back out. We're in good company—a lot of people feel taunted by this giant. An exorbitant amount of prescriptions in the developed world are written for worry, stress, anxiety, despair, and terror—all cousins of fear. People in the Western world take more medication to sleep at night than the rest of the world takes in a lifetime. The medications aren't all the same. Some people get their medication from a doctor, and some people get their medication from a bottle. But the end goal is always the same. We want to take the edge off. We want to decompress. We just want to forget about the things that are troubling us for a while. We want to not be afraid.

The answer is seldom as simple as saying, "Fear, go away in Jesus' name." Fear is a symptom of a deeper cause. We need to dig down and get to the root of the matter. Actually, there are at least three roots. Three causes. Three down-deep reasons that fear evidences in our lives. Let's examine these three roots, and ask Jesus to jar these loose from the ground of our hearts.

1. Fear comes from our conditioning.

Some people were raised in an environment of fear and worry. Maybe you were born into a family of worriers. Your mom is a grand champion worrier. Or your grandmother is. Maybe your father. Or your grandfather. You were barely out of the womb and family members were like, "Oh my gosh, don't drop the baby. Bundle her up tight. Make sure she's not too hot. Make sure she's not too cold. Make sure she's wearing a bicycle helmet. Make sure she's invested in the right 401K."

New parents get the jitters. That's fine. We see this in the new parents who come to our church, and it's okay. They want the best for their baby, and they want to do everything they can to ensure their child's safety. The parents are "vigilant" more than fearful, and vigilance is undoubtedly a good thing in today's culture.

But in other cases, people are raised in a genuine climate of fear. Life is treated like one big threat that never diminishes. At any minute, something could go wrong. And it probably will. The fear only progresses as a child gets older. One domino falls, and then another. After awhile, the fear in a person's life feels like a chain of constantly falling dominoes. A person's whole life gets built on shaky ground.

My dad could worry with the best of them, a trait that annoyed me when I was younger. Now that I am *past* Dad's age when I was a teenager, I'm not laughing anymore. Like so many of his characteristics (good and not-so-good), I see fruit of those very same traits ripening in my life.

2. Fear comes from our concealing.

Any time we conceal something major under the hood of our lives, fear is allowed to flourish. This is the pattern: We make mistakes. We sin. But we don't confess. Mostly because we feel embarrassed. Or we feel ashamed. Or we don't want to be thought of as anything less than perfect.

So we choose to keep going in the same stressful direction, living with the horrible feeling that someday whatever we've done will become public knowledge. We stuff those feelings of shame or embarrassment or perfectionism deep within us, and the stuffed feelings worm their way out of us in the form of anxiety. What if the real "us" gets revealed? What if we mess up again? What will everybody think?

Concealing will drive us crazy. Mistakes and sins and imperfections were never meant to be bottled up. We need to shed those feelings of impending doom at the foot of the cross.

3. Fear comes from our controlling.

Some people want to control everything. The outcome of circumstances, the outcome of conversations, the outcome of other people's lives. They soon realize that much of life can't be controlled—particularly how other people act. So fear, stress, worry, and anxiety are born.

Do you know controlling people? They try to run not only their lives but the lives of everyone around them.

The antidote
to fear is
faith, and the
soundtrack
of faith is
worship.

As a controller, you really do go crazy, because you fear all the things you can't control. What if something doesn't turn out the way I want it to? What if somebody messes up the plan I've worked so hard for? What if somebody doesn't cooperate with all the outcomes I want?

Ask yourself this: What in your life have you truly ever controlled?

Your Relentless Giant

It's helpful for us to spend time before the Lord and be honest about what's deep in our hearts. Are any of those three roots present? Sometimes we can have a cocktail of all three. If we have conditioning and concealing and we're controlling, then we're probably taking some medication.

Fortunately, it doesn't need to be that way. We don't need to accommodate the giant of fear. When we go beneath the surface to discover the root of fear, that's a good place to start. By the power of God in us, we examine that root and bring it to Jesus and flow Scripture over it and through it. We immerse ourselves in the goodness and greatness of God, and let Jesus shine his light on that root.

As you've seen so far, in each chapter in this book we're going to examine another facet of the biblical account of David and Goliath. It's important that we not miss any of the details if we want to see our giants defeated.

Let's go back a little and look at 1 Samuel 17:4. It says, "A champion named Goliath, who was from Gath, came out of the Philistine camp." Stop right there, because there's something important in that phrase. The word *champion* means that Goliath had a record. He had a history, and that's significant because a lot of us have history with our giants. These giants didn't just show up this morning. They've been around for a while. Their track record becomes one of the taunts used against us. Ever heard one of these voices?

- *Remember when you went to that retreat and promised how your life was going to change? Guess what, it didn't.*
- *Remember that time you thought you were going to be all big and bold and you lit a candle by your bed before you went to sleep and said, "The light of God is with me"? Too bad, sucker. I still won out on that day.*
- *Remember that time you went to church and they had that message on life change, and you thought you felt something different that day? Nope, nothing changed. Won't then. Won't now.*

That's the voice of your Goliath.

When the Goliath of the Bible stepped out and faced the armies of Israel, his record was announced. It wasn't simply

Goliath. It was "Goliath the champion from Gath." The Philistines let everyone know he was a champion fighter. He was an undefeated warrior. He came from Gath, a territory of thugs. All that announcing of Goliath's history was part of the larger plan to demoralize the Israelites.

First Samuel 17:4–7 continues the description of Goliath: He was over nine feet tall. "He had a bronze helmet on his head and wore a coat of scale armor of bronze weighing five thousand shekels." That's 125 pounds of armor. Many of us couldn't lift 125 pounds, let alone carry it in a fight. But that's what this champ did. Scripture goes on to say, "On his legs he wore bronze greaves, and a bronze javelin was slung on his back. His spear shaft was like a weaver's rod, and its iron point weighed six hundred shekels." That's fifteen pounds—not the entire spear, but just the spear point. "His shield bearer went ahead of him."

The harassment had been going on for forty days and forty nights. Goliath came out every morning and every night. He started the day taunting, and he ended the day taunting. He started the day demoralizing and diminishing, and he ended the day demoralizing and diminishing. "Goliath stood and shouted to the ranks of Israel, 'Why do you come out and line up for battle?' . . . Choose a man and have him come down to me. If he is able to fight and kill me, we will become your subjects; but if I overcome him and kill him, you will become our subjects and serve us.' Then the Philistine said, 'This day I defy the armies of Israel!'" (vv. 8–10). In other words, "I defied you yesterday, and the day before and the day before and the day before and the day before and the day before, and I'm doing it again today."

Giants are relentless. They don't take days off.

Check out verse 11. It sums up exactly what giants do to us. "On hearing the Philistine's words, [King Saul] and all the Israelites were dismayed and terrified."

Fast-forward to verses 20–24 where we see another situation developing.

> Early in the morning David left the flock in the care of a shepherd, loaded up and set out, as [his father] had directed. He reached the camp as the army was going out to its battle positions, shouting the war cry. Israel and the Philistines were drawing up their lines facing each other. David left his things with the keeper of supplies, ran to the battle lines and asked his brothers how they were. As he was talking with them, Goliath, the Philistine champion from Gath, stepped out from his lines and shouted his usual defiance, and David heard it. Whenever the Israelites saw the man, they all fled from him in great fear.

Can you imagine what that must have been like? Chances are, we've been in the midst of a righteous army that lifts a war cry but remains immobilized by the taunts of the Enemy. That's what some churches look like today. We gather each Sunday and lift up powerful anthems of worship to our God. That's our war cry. We position ourselves for battle. We claim the victory. We might even shout down the Devil. But then that's as far as we ever get. When the Sunday service is over, the same giant steps up and defies the power of God to keep us and save us and transform us.

For a lot of us, we settle into a dual existence, a schizophrenic faith. One part of us fully believes in the rule and reign of Jesus, confident he is able to change things for the better. The other part of us accommodates the "pet tiger," caves in to the giant, and lives in the valley of defeat. Sadly, this is the norm for a lot of us.

But all of us can hear the taunts:

- *You're too small. You can't do it.*
- *You're too weak to overcome anything.*
- *History is against you.*
- *I'm undefeated. You don't have a chance.*
- *You're just like your mom . . . your dad . . . your sister . . . your brother.*
- *This will always be a part of your life.*
- *You can't change.*
- *Get used to it. Your life will always be this way.*
- *Face it, deep down, you don't even want to be different.*

What's the solution?

The solution is not more determination. The solution is faith. Our giants can taunt us, but they don't have ultimate power.

Jesus has the ultimate power. Jesus builds up our faith, and faith is the antidote to fear. Faith is saying, "I have confidence in God that he is bigger than this giant."

I love Romans 10:17. The specific context of this verse has to do more with salvation, but we can lay it over the topic of fear too. It says, "Faith comes by hearing, and hearing by the word of God" (NKJV). When we see and hear God in and through his Word, the Word allows us to hear that Jesus is enough and to see that God is bigger. That builds up our faith, and our faith becomes the stone that shuts up the giant that's already defeated, the giant called fear. When we hear and see Jesus, things change in our lives.

So our invitation is to never take our focus off of Jesus. The apostle Peter did that. More than once, actually. Remember what happened to him during the storm on the sea?

Caught in the Storm

In Matthew 14:22–33, Jesus sent his disciples out onto the Sea of Galilee while he stayed behind because he'd had a long day. A big crowd had been following him, and now he just wanted to be alone with his Father. He said to his disciples, "I got an idea. You guys go ahead, I'll catch up with you later." They agreed, so Jesus went up on the mountain to pray in a quiet and solitary place.

When evening came, the disciples were out in the middle of the lake and a storm came up.

It was no small storm. The wind howled. Whitecaps crested the waves. The boat was tossed about. It was one of those storms where they weren't certain they were going to make it to safety again. That's when Jesus decided to walk out to his disciples on the water. The storm had raged for hours, and it was far into the night by then, shortly before dawn. Jesus walked right on top of the waves. Verses 26–27 give us more of the story: "When the disciples saw him walking on the lake, they were terrified. 'It's a ghost,' they said, and cried out in fear. But Jesus immediately said to them: 'Take courage! It is I. Don't be afraid.'"

Peter, all big and bold, said, "Lord, if it's you . . . tell me to come to you on the water" (v. 28).

Jesus said, "Come" (v. 29).

Can you imagine that? The visibility wasn't great. The waves and water and darkness were raging all around. But Peter looked toward the voice and stepped out onto the water. He started walking toward Jesus. Verse 30 says, "But when [Peter] saw the wind, he was afraid and, beginning to sink, cried out, 'Lord, save me!'"

Notice how Peter "saw" the wind. I have friends who sail, and they describe how the gusts of a windstorm will actually create dark corduroy-like ripples on top of the waves. You can see and hear and feel a gust of wind as it moves down the lake. A storm is a multisensory experience, similar to how the giant of fear can attack us. We feel fear in the pit of our stomach, in the clamminess of our hands. We hear fear in the negative self-talk we use. We see fear as a situation plays out either in our minds or in front of our eyes. What Peter experienced through all of those senses contributed to him being immobilized by fear. Look at verses 30–31. He began to sink and "cried out, 'Lord, save me!' Immediately Jesus reached out his hand and caught him. 'You of little faith,' he said, 'why did you doubt?'"

The answer is obvious. Hello? The swells were fourteen feet tall. The gusts of wind were pummeling Peter. Sheets of water flew over him. And then there was the whole walking-on-water thing. Peter realized for a second he didn't normally do that. I'm sure the picture of him drowning flashed through his mind.

But there is good news. As soon as Peter said, "Lord, save me," immediately Jesus grabbed him. There was no hesitation. No delay. It says "immediately." Jesus was closer to Peter than he thought.

The storm didn't stop immediately—that happened after Peter and Jesus reached the boat. No, the storm was still raging when Jesus caught Peter. On the way to the boat, I think Jesus probably said to Peter—just like Jesus says to us, "It's okay. I've got you—even in the midst of this storm. You have nothing to fear."

The Stuff of Faith

What do we need to hear and see and feel and understand about Jesus that replaces what the giants are saying to us? Four things.

1. We remind ourselves that God is able.

God is able. Period. That's what we need to constantly remind ourselves of.

It may take some time for us to weave this into the fabric of our thinking, sure. We may have worked our way into a big giant mess of fear and anxiety and stress over months and even years, so it may take some time to peel away the layers so this giant is removed. But it may happen instantaneously too.

God can work instantaneously. In fact, by the power of the name of the Lord Jesus Christ of Nazareth, somebody can be broken free from the chains of the giant of fear right here and now, this very moment as you're reading this book. You can shut the cover and never be demoralized by that giant again.

Yet God often works through a process. Lazarus came alive in an instant, but he still needed to walk out of that grave (John 11). The people around him still needed to unwrap his grave clothes. The layers may need to come off you as well. Maybe that involves seeking medical help for a season. Maybe you need to walk through some life situations with a trusted counselor who loves Jesus and who's ten years ahead of you in the journey. Maybe a trusted friend or a small group needs to step in and help you while God superintends the process.

No matter what the process is, it begins with confession. Our words are powerful. And the opening confession is more of a declaration than anything. It's this: my God is able to save.

Do you know where this idea comes from? Read through the last several chapters of Isaiah, starting around chapter 46, and you'll see the limitless ability of God laid out for his people. God reminds us again and again that he always has a plan. He's bigger than anything the world can throw at us. We might grow afraid. We might start wondering if a problem will ever be solved, or we might become fearful because we don't know the outcome. But God reminds us that he is God and there is no other God besides him.

That's where faith develops—when we lean into those truths.

As I've mentioned, during a dark stretch in my life, when fear dominated the day and absolutely owned the night, I ended up in an emergency room under a doctor's care for extreme depression-triggered anxiety. For a brief season I needed medication to help rewire and reboot my brain. Medication, I have since learned, is a norm in the struggle against anxiety and depression for more people than I ever imagined.

One day I asked the doctor, "How does this drug work? Why does it make me feel calmer?"

"Do you understand how your cache works in your computer?" he asked. "And how you regularly need to refresh your cache to optimize your computer's speed and performance?"

I nodded.

"Your brain has a cache too," he said. "The medication erases what's in your short-term memory so your brain forgets for a moment what you were afraid of."

That's brilliant. And also why when you're on that medication you leave cabinet doors open and water running in the sink.

But what a powerful idea. Our body knows we need to refresh our memory banks to alleviate fear. That's exactly how God's Word works. As we soak and meditate on his words, we replace in our brain what we are afraid of. A storm might be raging around us. A giant might be taunting us and demoralizing us. But we can saturate ourselves in the truths of God's Word and remind ourselves that God is able. He is always able. He is the Lord, and there is no other who can save but him. What he has purposed will happen, and what he has said will come about.

In Matthew 6:25–34, Jesus put the same idea into a little more user-friendly terms. He asked,

Why do you worry about what you'll eat? Why do you worry about what you'll wear? Why do you worry about your clothes? Don't you know that your father in heaven knows what you need? He's clothed the lilies of the field in all their beauty. Not a bird falls from the sky without his knowledge.

He gives to everything on this earth what they have. Surely he, your father, will give you what you need. For who of you by worrying can add one inch of comfort to your life? Your father will give you what you need because he is able. (author's paraphrase)

2. We set the Lord always before us.

I love Psalm 16, written by the shepherd boy, David, whom God used to show us the picture of Jesus killing Goliath. The whole psalm is great to memorize, but if that seems too much right away, just commit this one verse to memory: Psalm 16:8. David said, "I have set the LORD always before me; because he is at my right hand, I shall not be shaken" (ESV).

Isn't that great?! Why did David not feel terrorized by the giant? Because David constantly fixed his focus on someone bigger than Goliath—that's why David wasn't afraid of him. David set the Lord always before him. Because God was at David's right hand, David would not be shaken.

The giant was bigger than David. But God was bigger than the giant.

This verse is a terrific reminder that God is present in our lives too. The term *right hand* in the Old Testament indicated a valued, honored, and even intimate position. If you sat at the right hand of someone, then that was the best seat in the house. In the New Testament, the equivalent for believers is that Jesus lives in us. We are crucified with Christ, and we no longer live, but Christ lives in us (Galatians 2:20). Jesus lives in us when giants taunt us. Jesus lives in us when we are in the midst of a storm. Because Jesus is at our right hand, we will not be shaken.

Psalm 16 doesn't end there. It shows us the results of maintaining our focus on Christ. Verse 9 says, "Therefore my heart is glad and my tongue rejoices; my body also will rest secure."

That giant has fallen, my friends. God is able. He is always able. Our invitation is to set him before us always. To not take our eyes off him. With faith we can say our hearts are glad, and our tongues rejoice, and our bodies will rest secure.

3. We name what's keeping us up at night.

I have learned that anxiety can be devastating, but I've also come to understand that anxiety is not a thing in and of itself. In other words, if someone says, "Pray for me, my *anxiety* is acting up," what do they really mean? Saying, "I struggle with worry, or anxiety, or fear" doesn't get to the root of the problem. And until we are dealing with the root, we will never change the fruit.

We are anxious for a reason. Something, or someone, is making us anxious. To be free from fear we have to specifically name the things that are keeping us up at night.

"God, this is what is making me afraid:

"This bill that's coming due (for $916.95), and the fact I cannot pay it.

"(Bob) at work, and the fact that he is promoting (Amanda),

even though her work is not as good as mine, simply because he likes her.

"My daughter is with a guy (name him) I don't trust.

"The first chemo treatment is at 10:00 A.M. tomorrow with Dr. Oneida, and I am afraid of the outcome."

Once we identify the culprit and admit that our unrest is tied to this person or circumstance, we can off-load those cares to God. We can figuratively place them in our heavenly Father's hands, and we can trust them to his sovereign care. We don't minimize the situation; we maximize our view of the only One we can totally trust. We don't simply deny the problem we are threatened by; we relocate it to the hands of the only One who can manage it well. And we leave it there as we close our eyes to sleep.

Like David, we say:

> O Lord, how many are my foes!
> Many are rising against me;
> many are saying of my soul,
> "There is no salvation for him in God."
> But you, O Lord, are a shield about me,
> my glory, and the lifter of my head.
> I cried aloud to the Lord,
> and he answered me from his holy hill.
> I lay down and slept;
> I woke again, for the Lord sustained me. (Psalm 3:1–5 ESV)

4. We fill our mouths with praise.

Notice again that trifecta of goodness in Psalm 16:9: "Therefore my heart is glad and my tongue rejoices; my body also will rest secure."

When Jesus is in view, worship can flow unobstructed from our mouths. A song of praise can be on our lips. Seeing Jesus makes our hearts glad and restores rest. And seeing Jesus causes us to sing.

But why would we sing when the circumstances are what they are? When the outcome is not yet decided?

We sing because we see God. We see his might and are reminded of his love. We remember that he has always come through for us and that his mercy has never failed us. We don't wave a magic wand over whatever is causing us to fear and have it instantly disappear. We simply relegate our fear to its proper place, on the other side of Jesus in our view. We don't lose sight of Jesus because of the raging storm; we momentarily lose sight of the wind and the waves because of Jesus. With eyes fixed on Jesus we cry out, "You are in control!" We do not ignore the presence of danger. We declare the presence of our God.

Worship and worry cannot occupy the same space; they can't both fill our mouths at the same time. One always displaces the other. We either speak doom and destruction, kicking into high gear our worrying and stressing. Or we recount the size and character of the Almighty. We release our outcomes to him and center our thinking in his sovereign plans.

The antidote to fear is faith, and the soundtrack of faith is worship.

God encourages us to *put on* the garment of praise when we feel entangled by the spirit of heaviness. He gives us songs in the night, anthems for the dark night of the soul where worry and stress and fear lurk about. Our invitation is to preload our journey with playlists of worship. Sing into the face of the uncertainty about a sure and unchanging God.

We have the ability to determine where we look and to whom we look. We're called to set Jesus in view, especially when the battle rages.

When You're Lost in a Store

Can you remember what it feels like to "rest secure"?

That's the indication that the giant of fear has fallen, isn't it? Picture back to when you were a kid. You were with your mom in a store, and you were getting old enough that she didn't need to hold your hand all the time. You were just gaining the freedom to explore and roam, so you went a few feet away and that was all right; then you went a few more feet away, and that was all right. You could still see her. Then you went a few more feet away. You were feeling pretty good about yourself then. Four years old and really independent. Checking out the shoe section all by yourself. But then you turned to look for your mom and suddenly you couldn't see her anywhere. Remember that feeling?

Uh . . . "Mom?"

You called a little louder, "MOM?"

Still nothing.

You started to move. You looked up. You looked down. You looked left. You looked right. Your heart started to beat hard and you were not far away from a meltdown. You rushed down one aisle. You rushed up another. "Mom? MOM?" *Where can she be?!*

You dropped to the floor and scanned desperately for her shoes beneath the racks.

Then you just let loose and wailed. You were crying because you felt lost and scared. You were crying because you lost sight of the one who cares for you. And then you heard it.

She called your name.

"Over here, baby," she said.

She knew where you were. She was watching for you. Waiting for you. Wanting you to refocus and put your eyes back on her.

That's what it feels like to rest secure. We are found again. We're right where we're supposed to be.

And this is our invitation from God—to constantly be aware of his presence. To reestablish our focus on Jesus. When we deliberately and purposely focus our attention on Christ, we are reminded that God is able. We know he is always present with us. And we also know he is always good. We say with David, "I have set the Lord always before me. Because he is at my right hand, I will not be shaken."

Do we want to combat the fear in our lives? The battle is not ours. The battle belongs to the Lord. Jesus has already taken the sling and the stone and slain the giant. The giant of fear has already fallen. The work is already done by Christ on the cross. Our responsibility is to have faith. That's the antidote. God is able. Jesus is enough. When we set our eyes on him, we will not be shaken. We will rest secure.

But maybe fear isn't your nemesis. Maybe it's something else.

CHAPTER 4

Rejection Must Fall

—

Rejection is real.

None of us want to feel like we aren't good enough. Or smart enough. Or wanted enough.

Nobody wants to be left out or looked over.

We may put on an exterior that says *we don't need anyone else's approval.* But, even in saying that, aren't we kind of admitting that we do?

As much as we wish it wasn't so, the opinions of others matter. A word of rejection, even something small that wasn't even aimed to really hurt us, can stick and sting.

For some of you, the fact that you actually were rejected is a constant companion. It's like a cold wind that follows you wherever you go. Some form of rejection in the past has festered with time and riddled you with insecurity, insignificance, and a sense of abandonment.

Maybe your father didn't stick around to even meet you.

Or your spouse walked out the door and is now living in Seattle with another woman and her two kids.

Or your parents split and you've had to adjust to a life of being shuttled between families.

Or a trusted friend stopped taking your calls and responding to your texts.

Or a loved one suddenly died and left you alone.

Your sense of rejection could be big.

Or it could be more subtle—a sense of inadequacy stemming from something seemingly harmless at the time.

When I was a teenager, I dreamed of becoming a professional tennis player. High school was all about practicing. Every day we hit tennis balls. We hit tennis balls in the winter. We hit tennis balls in the rain. We hit tennis balls in the heat. We hit tennis balls late at night. We hit tennis balls up against the side of a wall. We hit tennis balls all the time.

In my senior year, I did okay in singles and even made the number-one-ranked doubles team for our school. I could hold my own in doubles, but the real reason we were number one is because I had the best player on our team as my doubles partner. Ray Dukes and I were neighbors and good friends, and Ray Dukes was unquestionably the best at our school. His Arthur Ashe-model composite Head tennis racket was as smooth as his backhand.

Now, if you've got a doubles partner who's the best, then

You are worth *Jesus* to God.

you're going to be hard to beat as a team, because one great player can make a big difference in succeeding in doubles. Ray and I battled all spring long. We won our district match and made it to the regional tennis tournament. After a day of hard play, we found ourselves in the regional finals. This was big. If we won this match, then we'd go to state.

In the middle of the match I looked up and saw that my dad had suddenly appeared. He was leaning up against the building where the pro shop was, watching me. That was huge because my dad had never come to see me play tennis before. My dad loved me a lot—that wasn't the reason. He didn't have much flexibility in his work schedule and our matches were always in the afternoon. But here we were in the middle of the regional finals, and there was my dad. He'd never seen me play at this level before. His nickname for me was Ace (not related to tennis; he just liked the name, and I did too), and I was serving at the very moment I spotted my dad. I figured it must be a sign from God, because I was about to blow my opponent away with my best serve.

In tennis, you get two chances to serve each point. You want to put a ton of pace on your first serve, because if you fault (miss), it's okay, no pressure; you get a second serve. On your second serve you back off slightly and make sure the ball's completely under control, because if the second serve doesn't go in, then it's your opponent's point. A double fault.

I knew exactly what I was going to do. With my first serve, I was going to reach back and drive the ball so hard it would leave a convincing *thud* in the fence. In fact, I was going to go "up the T," which meant my serve would skim across the net flat, hard, low, and up the center line. My opponent wouldn't even see the ball, much less touch it. It was going to be so great. My dad was going to see me make this awesome serve, and he was going to think, *Wow, who knew? That's my kid. Way to go, Ace!*

Every good player begins a serve with the same routine. My routine was to bounce the ball three times on the court. *In the name of the Father, in the name of the Son, in the name of the Holy Spirit.* Just kidding, although looking back it couldn't have hurt. I bounced the ball three times, tossed it high overhead, and gave it everything. *Bam!*

Ten feet over the back line. Out.

A bead of sweat dripped off my forehead. The court seemed to have shrunk to the size of a matchbox. I swallowed hard and didn't dare look my father's direction. Again I did my routine. Three bounces. *Smack!*

Straight into the bottom of the net. Double fault.

Point for the other team.

I tried to shake it off and regroup on the next serve, but to little avail.

Serve after serve. Fault. Double fault. Net. Out. Conservatively, I bet I double-faulted ten times that day. It was brutal. Once in that match I double-faulted an entire game.

The only good news? Somehow we fought and clawed and

ended up winning the match. We were going to the state tennis tournament in doubles after all.

We were pumped.

How Do You Like My Insecure-gram?

————

Later that night, after we hit some *more* tennis balls following the match, I was eager to get back home and share the victory with my dad. He had to get back to the office right after we won and I hadn't had a chance to talk to him. I pictured him glancing my way when I came home and saying, "Hey, tough match. But you kept playing your guts out. Way to go. You're going to state. I'm proud of you, Ace."

Yet things never turn out quite like we plan.

My dad ended up coming home after me, and when he walked through our front door I was sitting across the room ready for a little celebration. But instead he kind of chuckled and said, "Well, I don't think we can call you Ace anymore. From now on we're going to call you Double Fault." He said it with a smile on his face. I think he meant it in the best way he could, because I smiled and laughed along too.

But it stung.

It genuinely stung. The really crazy part of that story is I played tennis competitively for years afterward; and although I don't play much anymore, there are times to this day when I go to serve the ball that I can hear my father's words in the back of my mind:

We're going to call you Double Fault.

I know someone is thinking, *Seriously, you're going to try to tell me that your dad made a snide remark and that was a big issue for you? Wow, what a wimp.*

I get it. For some of you the rejection is like Everest. Real. Raw. Consequential. And devastating.

I'm not saying getting a sarcastic remark for almost double-faulting the match away is the same as being abandoned by your parents on the doorstep of the hospital.

This story is about more than a kid playing tennis. It's about how the giant of rejection can grow in a person's mind and heart. I guarantee you my dad didn't have any intention of rejecting me that night. Nope, he was an amazing dad. His words were innocent in intent. After all, I had double-faulted—*a lot!*

But even when the intention is not harmful, a tiny seed of rejection can take root and wreak havoc in seasons to come.

Maybe right away when you hear the word *rejection* you go, "Yep, that's me. I totally understand what he's talking about, because I feel rejection all the time." But maybe the giant isn't that obvious in your life. Maybe you say, "Well, I get that rejection can be a problem for some people, but it's not for me. I'm pretty successful, so I'll just sit this one out."

Keep reading—because rejection shows up in more ways than we think. This giant has cousins on both sides of the family—and the two sides don't look anything alike.

On one side of the family, the cousins are called insecurity, low self-esteem, low self-worth, inferiority, and even self-hate.

On the other side of the family—and it can be surprising to learn these are related—the cousins are called driven to succeed, perfectionism, winning at all costs, and being an overachiever.

Both sets of behavior are part of the same dysfunctional family. If you've been told you're worthless, then you think low of yourself. And if you've been told you're only valuable when you perform, then you think you've got to prove yourself every single time to be accepted. Both methods of coping are signs you're battling the giant of rejection.

All people battle with some sort of rejection. We've all felt that we don't measure up. We all experience performance-based environments where we feel we need to work hard or else we won't gain approval.

Way back in the garden of Eden, a seed of rejection was planted in humanity. That seed is a big spiky plant now, and its blooms insist we must compare ourselves with everybody else. See, we all began miraculously—fully loved and fully accepted—in the mind and heart of almighty God. We are all God's creations. Masterpieces. Yet we were born into a fallen world that's bought the lie that people are only worth what they can achieve or what other people say they are worth.

Back in Genesis 3, Adam and Eve lived in the garden of Eden in perfect harmony. At their inception, they awakened to the love and wonder in the eyes of their Maker. God walked with them closely and intimately every day. Adam and Eve lived unspoiled lives in an unadulterated environment. But then the serpent, the embodiment of evil, entered the story and insisted that Adam and Eve needed something else to be happy. God was withholding something from Adam and Eve, the serpent lied, and their lives were lacking.

Adam and Eve's answer to the serpent should have been, "No way. God's not withholding anything good from us. We are created in God's image. We have the stamp of divinity in our hearts. Only humans have this. The plants don't have this. The animals don't have this. Even the stars in the sky don't have this. But people do. We've been made in the likeness of God" (see Genesis 1:26–27).

But Adam and Eve didn't say this. They listened to Satan. They disobeyed God, and when that happened, sin entered the world. A seed was planted called rejection. This seed causes people to think there's something inferior about us—there's something else we need to be everything we could be.

We see signs of this everywhere today. The fallen world we live in is corrupted by a sense of inferiority. We learn early in life to compare ourselves with everybody else. We start looking around at others to figure out how we're doing. This is particularly troubling in today's modern world where social media is in our faces all day long.

When I was a kid, I went to an elementary school where there were maybe twenty other kids in my class. Twenty-five at the most. That's basically all the people I had to compare myself to. But today, thanks to social media, we've got an uncountable number of people to compare ourselves to. The entire world is up for comparison. Every time a person posts on social media, that person is basically asking, "How do I measure up, world? Do you like me or not?" If we're not careful it can become a comparison trap.

When do you get the "likes"? It's an "only if" situation. Only if your hair looks amazing, only if you went to the concert, only if you ate at the latest, greatest restaurant, only if you went to the right conference, only if you got the best recognition, only if you're hanging out with the coolest or most famous person, only if you're vacationing on the right beach, only if your kids are cute enough, only if your girlfriend or boyfriend is a "babe" (or bae if you don't have time for the extra "b"), only if your DYI project turned out spectacular—then and only then will you get the "likes." Hello, world, this is me—do you like me?

Only if.

We don't post a selfie when our face is covered with a big breakout of zits. No, we don't post too many selfies of the real world. "Hey, world, I just woke up. My hair is greasy and there's gunk in the corner of my eyes!" You don't see that on your feed too frequently, if ever. We don't post selfies that show when our hair style went wrong, when we eat at the dud restaurant, when we come in third (or don't get recognized at all), when we're hanging out with the ordinary Joes, when that do-it-yourself coffee table made of reclaimed wood looks like an ugly disaster only fit for the dump. I mean, sure, we take selfies sometimes to talk about what a bad day we've had. Sometimes we mock our failures. Or we complain on social media. But usually even then we're fishing for a compliment. We want a boost of encouragement. We want people to agree with us, to side with us in our frustration, to say, "Oh, you poor baby, that ugly table is actually better than you think."

Social media can be a good thing when used well. But if social media is the place we get our value, then we're sunk. If we live for people's approval, we will die by their rejection.

If we are not careful, then we will forget we were miraculously created by God for a purpose and a plan that he set in motion for our lives. He didn't ask us to compare ourselves to other people or run someone else's race. He said, "Run your race." Period. He didn't ask us to work on someone else's timetable. He wants us to work on *his* timetable. God wants us to believe and know in our souls that "he who began a good work in [us] will carry it on to completion until the day of Christ Jesus" (Philippians 1:6). Jesus wants us to understand where we came from and whose we are. When we lose sight of our miraculous beginnings, and our re-creation in the beauty of the person of Christ, then we're going to be taunted and tormented by this giant of rejection all the days of our lives.

We Are the Work of God

David, when he came to the battle against Goliath, was up against the giant of rejection. It's right there in our text.

At this time, David was still a teenager. He wasn't in the army; he was taking supplies to his brothers. When he got to the camp, he heard about Goliath. He heard the taunting and didn't like what he heard. He asked who this giant was and who was going to take him down. But his brother didn't appreciate his inquisitiveness. Note the text: "When Eliab, David's oldest brother, heard him speaking with the men, he burned with anger at him and asked, 'Why have you come down here?'" (1 Samuel 17:28).

Let's back up a step, because this response from Eliab isn't surprising if we know the rest of the story. In 1 Samuel 16, we see that David had seven older brothers. The prophet Samuel came to Jesse's house to anoint a new king for Israel. Jesse was David's father, and Samuel asked Jesse to bring him all his sons. Jesse started with the oldest, Eliab. Eliab came out, and he was the biggest, oldest, and strongest. Surely he was going to be the new king. But Samuel said, "Nope. Not him."

How about the next oldest brother?

Nope, not him either.

The next?

Nope.

And on down the line. David was so young that Jesse didn't bother bringing him in at first. David was out in the field tending sheep. But Samuel asked to see him. And when David arrived, Samuel said, "That's the one. Anoint him."

How do you think Eliab felt that day? Undoubtedly he was jealous and spurned. The system seemed upside down. He wasn't chosen as king. The youngest brother was. The kid who wasn't even in the lineup at first.

For us, this is a good reminder that God works in his own way. It is not by the strength of men that battles are won. It is by the work of God. That's why in the story of David and Goliath we've uncovered the huge revelation that we are *not David*. It's not about us gathering our slings and stones and going down to kill the giant of rejection ourselves. No, God is going to do that for us. He chooses the weak things to confound the strong, the simple things to upend the wise.

In this case God chose the youngest of all, as a way of showing it's not the outward appearance that impresses God. It's a heart of faith.

In a perfect world, Eliab would have understood this. When David showed up at the battle, Eliab would have been proud of him, not put off by him. Eliab would have said, "Hey, everybody, this is my little brother. He's going to be the king of Israel one day. I get to be the older brother of the king of Israel—isn't that amazing?" Then Eliab would turn to David and be the big brother God called him to be. Eliab would say, "Man, I'm glad you're here, David. Thanks for coming. Thanks for the bread and cheese."

Inspired, Eliab could have offered to fight to protect his brother. At the least, he could have encouraged David when his younger brother said he wanted a shot at Goliath.

But that's not what happened. Eliab was still bitter. He felt like he'd been rejected, so he burned with anger and said to David, "Why have you come down here? And with whom did you leave those few little sheep in the wilderness? I know how conceited you are and how wicked your heart is; you came down only to watch the battle" (1 Samuel 17:28). Eliab felt rejected, and rejected people reject people. If you feel rejected, or you genuinely were rejected, it's likely you are passing on your sense of rejection to those around you.

Fast-forward thirteen years from the night my nickname was almost changed to Double Fault. My dad had been disabled by a vicious brain infection that left him mentally and physically disabled. And the aftereffects of the trauma of the disease and several brain surgeries had accelerated the aging process. Dad started saying things I'd never heard him say before. He was talking without a filter, like older people sometimes do.

I knew he'd had a rough childhood. His parents separated, and I'd heard he had lived with his aunt for a while, maybe had been shuffled back and forth between a few different relatives. But I didn't ask and he didn't talk about it. Turns out I didn't know the half of it. One day, sitting alone in his hospital room, I was telling my dad how much I loved him. And how much Jesus did too.

"No one has ever loved me," he replied, a deep sadness in his eyes. "No one ever wanted me."

I froze in my seat, tears immediately brimming in my eyes.

Instantly, so much of life (even the chippy "Double Fault" remark) made total sense. My dad, the invincible hero I'd looked up to my whole life (and still do even though he's gone), was smashed in the dirt of rejection at the outset of his life and he never fully recovered.

My dad wasn't trying to reject me, yet the aftershocks of his own rejection were uncontrollably reverberating from the real rejection he had endured.

The second time David felt rejected was after he said he wanted to fight the giant. King Saul heard about it and brought David in to talk to him. Saul said to David, "You are not able to go out against this Philistine and fight him; you are only a young man, and he has been a warrior from his youth" (v. 33). In other words, "Hey, David, you're not good enough. You're not big enough. You're not strong enough. You're not capable of this."

We've all felt this, although maybe the messages were said to us differently.

"You're never going to do that."

"Don't get any crazy ideas."

"Don't get your hopes up."

"You're never going to amount to anything."

"You're not smart enough."

"You're not talented enough."

"You're not beautiful enough."

"You're not worthy enough."

"You're not wanted enough."

David pressed through this and eventually went out to fight the giant, at which point he felt yet another rejection.

Goliath came closer to David, looked David up and down, and saw that "he was but a youth, ruddy and handsome" (v. 42 ESV). What does *ruddy* mean? It refers to the color in David's cheeks. He wasn't weathered like a rugged man yet. He was fresh-faced. And "[Goliath] despised [David]. He said to David, 'Am I a dog, that you come at me with sticks?' And the Philistine cursed David by his gods. 'Come here,' he said, 'and I'll give your flesh to the birds and the wild animals'" (vv. 43–44).

Are you kidding me?

First, David gets rejected because his older brother still feels rejected. Second, David gets rejected from Saul because David is too small. Third, David gets it from Goliath because he's just a rosy-cheeked kid. David just can't win. He gets it from all sides. The first and the last taunts, I think, were the hardest for David to hear. It's one thing to hear from the king that you're too small to wear his armor. The king was right. Saul was just trying to help out. But to be slighted by your older brother has got to be difficult. And then to be attacked by an enemy, basically for being *too cute* to fight, that's got to be hard to take too. An enemy will come at you with everything he's got. But why attack someone because they're too fresh-faced?

Rejection Takes Aim at Us All

No amount of money or looks or success can insulate you from the possibility of rejection. Rejection comes after all of us in differing ways.

Some of us have incredible potential, but we don't want to try anything bold because we don't want to fail. The easy choice: live in the relative safety of mediocrity because we think that's better than rejection.

At the other end of the spectrum are the people who are determined to win at everything, to prove to somebody that they are good enough, beautiful enough, worthy enough, wanted enough. They won't rest until they are the first in the class, the head of the organization, the most respected person in the group. But they're never happy because they're building up their self-worth based on their accomplishments. They don't know what they're going to do when their accomplishments aren't good enough anymore. It's the same giant of rejection.

Some of the most beautiful people in our culture are the most insecure. Some get judged by others because they look *too* beautiful. Others, despite their appearance, never felt worth much inside. I remember seeing this back in the days when Shelley and I led a campus ministry at Baylor. Some of the girls that looked like they had it all together would meet with Shelley and me after coming to our Bible study. They'd say things like, "I'm really struggling. Can you help? I have an eating disorder. I have an image problem. I am struggling with my self-worth and my value. I don't like the way I look."

It was surprising to hear. You take a step back and you're thinking, *Of all the people on this campus, what do you have to feel insecure about? You've got looks. You've got brains. You've got all the right clothes. You're in the right sorority. You're driving that super-cool BMW. You're the one everybody wants to be around. You're considered one of the most beautiful people at this school. Why are you insecure?*

You can find models who are the saddest people on the planet because of the giant of rejection. And it's not just models either. It's people at the top of every category. You find great athletes who feel insecure because they know they're only one injury away from losing their position on the team or their income stream. You find incredibly smart people who are insecure because they feel like people only like them for what they know. You find competent and capable people who feel like they've got an image to keep up. Or an image to try to create.

And the fear of rejection can lead you to some troubling places. Psychologists tell us that one of the most powerful forces in humanity is acceptance. It's what we all crave. That's why some of you have friends who are not good for you, but you hang around with them anyway. Because they accept you. They're not encouraging you to be all God wants you to be. They don't have the same value systems you have. But they accept you, and that's a powerful pull in your life. Some of you are dating somebody and you know they are not the right person for you. But the sense of acceptance this person is giving you is overwhelming your sense of what's best for you. That's how strong acceptance is. But is this true acceptance?

Of course not.

David pressed through the rejection he felt to go on and accomplish the purposes of God for his life. He arrived at the battle from a place of *true* acceptance. And this is God's invitation to us as well—to cloak ourselves in the true acceptance that Christ offers. Whether it's school or work or with our peers or family, we potentially face rejection every day. The only thing that will help us move past the giant of rejection is to immerse ourselves in the acceptance of Christ. We need to arrive at the battle already feeling accepted.

So how do we develop this confidence in his acceptance? We do it by embracing these four big principles.

1. We understand the miracle of our creation.

We clothe ourselves in acceptance when we understand we are the work of God. David knew that about himself. Under the inspiration of the Holy Spirit, David wrote Psalm 139. It's a beautiful psalm that helps order our lives day by day. Right in the middle of it, David declares, "For you created my inmost being; you knit me together in my mother's womb. I praise you because I am fearfully and wonderfully made; your works are wonderful, I know that full well" (vv. 13–14).

That's a mouthful of giant-slaying truth right there. We are each reverently and wonderfully made. God doesn't make mistakes. God doesn't make rejects—that comes from assembly-line lingo. When a reject comes down the line, a worker says, "That one's perfect. That one's perfect. That one's wrong. Oh no, not that one. Either throw it back and start over again or discard it." God doesn't do that.

David affirms this. Later in the same psalm he declares, "Your works are wonderful, I know that full well. My frame was not hidden from you when I was made in the secret place, when I was woven together in the depths of the earth. Your eyes saw my unformed body; all the days ordained for me were written in your book before one of them came to be" (vv. 14–16).

The giant of rejection does not want you to remember the miracle of your creation. For this giant to fall, for this giant to be rendered powerless in your life, immerse yourself in this fact:

God made you.

Uniquely.

Beautifully.

Intentionally.

Purposefully.

Wonderfully.

2. We revel in the mystery that Jesus chose us.

How do we develop true acceptance? We clothe ourselves in Christ's acceptance when we revel in the mystery of his choosing.

Ephesians 1 tells us how we got into the family of God. Beginning in verse 4, it says, "For he chose us in him before the creation of the world to be holy and blameless in his sight. In love he predestined us for adoption to sonship through Jesus Christ, in accordance with his pleasure and will—to the praise of his glorious grace, which he has freely given us in the One he loves."

That means from the very beginning of time, God chose you. Long before you knew him, he knew you. He loved you long before the world began. Before you ever felt the sting of rejection, God had already gone on record as choosing you. Before people decided whether or not you are good enough for them, God had already decided that he wanted to bring you into his family as a son or a daughter of almighty God.

Can you imagine that? If you are adopted, you may have struggled to some degree about your value or worth. And that's understandable. But the decision of an earthly parent cannot trump the choice God made when he fostered your creation in your mother's womb. Like the psalmist you can say, "Even if my father and mother abandon me, the LORD will hold me close" (Psalm 27:10 NLT).

If this is you, it might feel like your father and mother left you at the adoption agency and that is what defines you. But your heavenly Father had *already picked* you up before they ever dropped you off. Your heavenly Father said, "I choose you. I want you in my forever family—you are my daughter; you are my son. I give you a name—my name. I give you a place with me—and it's a place of love and abundance. I give you my inheritance, and my riches are limitless."

Before you were conceived, God went on record in the heavenlies and said, "I choose you as my own." That truth cultivates in us a sense of huge acceptance.

Hopefully, you have come to the place in life where you have chosen him too.

Yet Jesus chose us first (see John 15:16).

Let those words sink in.

Jesus chose us.

Jesus chose you.

3. We grasp how costly it was for Jesus to rescue us.

How do we develop true acceptance? We clothe ourselves in Christ's acceptance when we see the enormous cost God paid when he sent his Son to rescue us. It goes on to say in Ephesians 1:7–8, "In [Christ] we have redemption through his blood, the forgiveness of sins, in accordance with the riches of God's grace that he lavished on us."

The gospel isn't just a church talk. It's not just a good sermon. It tells every human what we need to know in the deepest part of our souls—that we have enormous worth to God. Faced with life without us, his choice was to allow his Son to die for us.

That's how he recovered us and rescued us.

God paid an enormous price for you.

There's a lot of talk in our country about what somebody's net worth is. We've got this list of the five hundred richest people in the world and the five hundred richest people in America. We can find out who's at the top and how many billions that person has.

We can discover their net worth—the sum of all their cash and assets on earth.

Now, if you're young, you may feel left out of the net worth conversation. You went to the ATM this morning, and you know exactly what your net worth is. It's $88.71. That's what the ATM told you, and you were pumped, because you needed fifty bucks and you had it in your account with change to spare. Hey, I've been there.

But if you are older, your financial picture has become more of a focal point. As we mature we are faced with questions about how much we have in the bank, how much equity we have in our house if we own one, how much is in our retirement funds, how our investments are doing right now.

But whether you are rich or poor, our net worth is not best reflected in dollars and cents or in what we own.

Our true net worth is Jesus Christ.

Our net worth is whose life was given for us.

Praise God for this, because another global financial crisis could come along any day. The wrong two countries could start a war tomorrow and our financial net worth could be cut in half. Who wants to live life on a plank that could disappear that fast? Our worth isn't wrapped up in what we achieve and accomplish, although we always seek to do our best. Our net worth is forever anchored in the fact that Jesus was given for us.

Sounds simplistic, I know. Yet it's powerful to walk through your day mindful of your true worth.

You are worth Jesus to God.

4. We live from acceptance, not for it.

Our giant of rejection is not going to fall until we admit that we desperately need acceptance. If you're too proud to say that, you most likely have some demons in your past that still might be lurking in the shadows. We were made to be accepted and embraced by our heavenly Father. We were made to be loved, for free.

The good news is that in Christ, we have everything we long for. Everything we need. We are not working to gain his acceptance. We already have it.

We live from his acceptance, not for the acceptance of others. Sure, we want to be loved and liked by others. And we want to love in a way that will allow us to hear from heaven, "well done." But we live as though we know we are already fully loved and accepted in him.

Just before the 2016 Summer Olympic Games began, I had the opportunity to lead a Bible study for some swimmers from the USA team. They were training in Atlanta, and I was asked to gather with them in a meeting room at a downtown hotel. I would only have a few minutes to share, as their schedules were extremely tight. Some of the swimmers still had a night training session to complete before their flight departed the next morning for Rio.

A swimmer who'd been to one of our Passion Conferences had invited me. Beyond that I wasn't completely sure who all the other athletes were in the room. I learned later there were multiple gold-medal-winning athletes and some aspiring swimmers who were headed to the Olympics for the first time. The morning before the event, I asked Jesus what he wanted me to share. I sensed the Spirit nudge my heart toward Matthew's gospel, chapter 3. *That's it,* I thought. I couldn't wait to get to the Bible study.

In the text, Jesus was thirty years old and ready to fulfill the mission that brought him to earth. On this day, he was baptized in the Jordan River to give us an example to follow. But then something powerful took place. "As soon as Jesus was baptized, he went up out of the water. At that moment heaven was opened, and he saw the Spirit of God descending like a dove and alighting on him. A voice from heaven said, 'This is my Son, whom I love; with him I am well pleased'" (vv. 16–17).

How amazing is that?

Jesus was at the beginning of his public ministry, yet his Father said he *already* loved him. Jesus hadn't given a message, healed anyone, walked on water, or died on the cross. Yet, his

Father was already pleased with him. God lavished his son with acceptance *before* he did a thing.

I was present in a circle of winners. These athletes had sacrificed their whole lives to compete and win. But winning won't guarantee that the giant of rejection doesn't still have a foot on our necks.

I said, "I don't know exactly what you've been trained to think just as you stand on the blocks ready for that beep that signals you into your race. Whatever you've been taught to think by your coaches, think that." I glanced at the head coach and he nodded and smiled. "But if you have a split second to spare, look down at that block and imagine the word *accepted* written on it with your name. Hear your heavenly Father saying for all to hear, 'This one is mine.' Imagine him whispering in your ear: 'I really, really love you. I am already pleased with you!'

"And then," I added, "swim your tail off! Not because acceptance is waiting for you at the end of the race—but because you already have it."

Pursue the One Who's Pursuing You

I love Psalm 8, another psalm of David. Although scholars debate the timing of its writing, some believe this psalm was written before David fought Goliath, when David was a young shepherd boy. This psalm talks about "the praise of children" (v. 2). It talks about "flocks and herds" and "the animals of the wild" (v. 7). All things that would have been common to David when he was young.

Just imagine David out in the fields at night, tending his flock by starlight. He wrote, "When I consider your heavens, the work of your fingers, the moon and the stars, which you have set in place, what is mankind that you are mindful of them, human beings that you care for them?" (vv. 3–4).

This is the biggest question of all time, isn't it? It might have been asked by David the teenager. It might have been asked by David the elderly king. We're not sure. But we do know that the psalmist is asking if humans have any significance. Why would God be mindful of us?

The answer is given subtly. David is looking up into the immensity of God's creation, yet he still knows he has a relationship with the One who made the sun and the moon and the stars and the heavens. He's blown away by God's indirect answer.

All this, yet God still cares for us.

All this, yet the God of the universe still knows our names.

All this, yet God has chosen us. He's made us his sons and daughters. He loves us. He cherishes us.

The psalm then talks about how God has crowned mankind with "glory and honor" (v. 5). It feels crazy to think the God of heaven knows us. The Creator of the universe knows who we are.

He has pursued us. He is in love with us. Think about how awesome this is. We freak out when we get thirty "likes" on a social media post. Yet the God of the universe is mindful of us!

David ends Psalm 8 with these words: "LORD, our Lord, how majestic is your name in all the earth!" (v. 9). Do you know why he concluded the psalm this way? It's because the worship of God shuts down the giants. Rejection and worship cannot exist in the same place. One displaces the other.

David didn't get puffed up about the fact that God knew his name. He turned his focus God-ward. It's like he was saying, "I know I'm loved, God, but what's really amazing, God, is how majestic you are!"

That's why our giants go down. Our freedom and God's glory are forever wound together in one story. Our giants go down so that we get free, yes, but they primarily go down so God gets glory.

Let's rediscover the miracle of our creation.

Let's revel in the mystery of God choosing us.

Let's wrap our hearts around the huge cost that was paid to rescue us, and turn our hearts toward the One who's already pursuing us.

But what about giants that don't even look like harmful things?

CHAPTER 5

Comfort Must Fall

—

Have you ever been tempted to postpone a commitment?

There was a time awhile back when Shelley and I needed to take an uncomfortable financial step. We'd gone to an event earlier in the year, and the theme of the conference was to lean into the global work and enterprise of God. I was one of the speakers at the conference, so my role was to align my talk with this theme and to encourage people to participate in what God was doing through generous financial gifts. It was cool for us personally, because whenever you get around a lot of people talking and praying about generosity and God's kingdom enterprise, you get inspired to be generous for God's kingdom enterprise.

That's what happened to Shelley and me. We wanted to join this work too. As the conference drew to a close, Shelley and I were talking with each other and I said, "Are you feeling something? I think God's tugging at my heart." And Shelley said, "I was just going to ask you the same thing, because God's tugging at my heart too." And I said, "I've got a specific number in mind I believe we should give," and Shelley said, "Me too." I told her my number and she told me hers and they both aligned and we were like, "Yeah, that's what we're going to do."

So we filled out the pledge form. We wanted to give as much as we were able, and we wrote down on paper the specific amount we committed to give and then turned in the card. The amount was pretty significant for us.

Things got interesting for us when, a short time after we got home from the conference, we got a letter in the mail encouraging us to fulfill our total pledge now. I did a double take. I had thought we could give the amount we'd pledged spread out over two years. Half this year. Half next year. But obviously I'd heard wrong, because conference organizers were asking us to fulfill the entire amount of our pledge right away. That was going to be much more difficult for us. I stared at the letter and began to process our options.

We were still committed to the kingdom purpose we were wanting to support—that wasn't the issue for us. Giving to God is an act of worship, and we were feeling it. We were thanking the Lord for letting us be a part of his plan. We were thankful that we weren't in debt up to our eyeballs and we had some available resources we could invest. We were happy that the conference organizers invited us to be part of the team and thrilled at what God was doing all over the world.

But the amount of money we needed to give all at once—that's what felt uncomfortable. We just needed to do the math and work out practically how we could make it happen.

You know how your joy can fade over time? A couple of weeks passed, and I didn't send in our pledge right away. I kept wondering if Shelley and I could give the full amount or not. I argued with myself. Maybe I hadn't been thinking straight at the conference—maybe we just got swept up in the emotion of it all. Maybe it wasn't God, after all. Maybe we could reduce the amount of our gift. Surely God would understand that I had misunderstood the time line, right?

I got out my calculator and started adding up our money, trying to figure things out a dozen different ways to make things work. Ever done that before? You're trying to mitigate against floating variables. Like, "Okay, if we give this here then we can do that, and if this happens then that will happen, and if this number moves then that number will move." Am I the only one who does this?

Right in the middle of all that planning and churning and wondering and worrying, I stopped. I absolutely stopped cold. Because within that frantic process I heard the still, small voice of God, and the word that God was impressing on my heart was this:

Fulfill what I led you to do, and do it now.
Stop adding things up.
Stop worrying.

Stop wondering how much stuff you need to have before you can actually step forward and obey me.

I am God and I've never let you down.

Every time I have led you to make a financial decision where you needed to trust me, you have always ended up saying, "Thank you, God, for leading us to do that."

There's never been a time in your life, married or single, when you've given to me and then looked back and said, "We regret giving to God what we gave to God."

I talked to Shelley and we agreed, "Let's not wait. Let's give the whole amount right now. Let's step out in faith and believe that God is big. Let's not work it out on paper first, because we *can't* work it out on paper. Let's let God work it out in our lives, and let's let his story become our story."

So we wrote the check for the full amount and sent it in. God wasn't calling us to be comfortable. He was calling us to be faithful.

Yet again, the struggle is real.

(I feel like I need to have a sidebar here, to encourage you that this chapter is not about who gives how much at what time. You need to do what God leads you to do as it relates to giving financially, and if you're not sure, ask for help from wise people in your life.)

The point is, most all of us desire to be comfortable, safe, secure. Yet comfortableness and obedience often butt heads.

Out of the Nest

I almost titled this chapter "Complacency Must Fall," because I understand how difficult it can be to think of comfort as a giant—something that taunts us and hurts our lives. I mean, usually comfort is a good thing, right? We like to provide a safe environment for our family. We like to kick back at the end of the day with our shoes off and watch a fun show on TV. We like hanging out in the backyard in a hammock. We like knowing how much money we've got in the bank and feeling financially secure. We like things to be orderly in our lives, not chaotic. We like things to be smooth and to go as planned. Isn't that comfort? Sure.

And none of those things are deadly in and of themselves.

Trouble arises when the desire for safety and security becomes the dominant theme of our lives. When a relaxation mentality supplants our attentiveness to God's call on our lives.

Jesus took time off, but he didn't come to earth to relax. He came for a specific mission and he left us with one as well.

That's why comfort is perhaps the scariest giant of them all. It's so subtle in its deception. It's the giant that causes us to miss the very best because we have settled for something good. On the surface everything looks fine. What could be wrong with having a good job? A nice family? A routine?

The problem is we might forget that in the grand scheme of

things (namely eternity), we have about five seconds on earth to make our lives count. *Really* count.

Here are a few specific ways comfort can become a harmful thing:

- *If we miss a great opportunity because we choose a safer, easier route.*
- If a good thing actually turns out to be harmful or counterproductive over time because it lulls us into a false sense of security.
- If we choose the good thing but miss the God-thing.
- If we buy into the idea that we work hard for a season of life and then we can choose to do whatever we want with the rest.
- If we slip into thinking it's "my life" to do with as I please.
- If my number one factor in deciding what I do is "whatever makes me happy."
- If comfort is sought ahead of everything else, including our desire to be available to God's plans.
- *If we grow accustomed to our sin and fail to confront it and remove it from our lives.*

That's the danger of comfort. That's why comfort can be such a deadly giant. I know how people can struggle with any number of overtly horrible things, but sometimes it's not the overtly horrible things that kill us. We aren't heroin addicts. We aren't going to prison for tax evasion. On the contrary, we are honest. And honorable.

Yet we have just settled for comfort, and the comfort ends up doing us in. Our abundant life on earth and our eternal reward in heaven aren't robbed by the "bad" stuff. Our chance for a meaningful life and a happy forever is robbed by comfort.

Each year on the side porch of our house where Shelley and I once lived, we had birds building nests. Sometimes it was a nuisance, but usually it was a good thing. A few springs back some birds built the biggest nest I'd ever seen. It was the size of a basketball. I wondered for a while if we had a bunch of squirrels living up there, but no, it was birds. We loved watching these birds work. I mean, sure their nest building was a little muddy and messy. But I have massive respect for birds, mother birds in particular. They build the nest. They sit on the eggs. They hatch the baby birds. They fly to and fro all day long collecting worms and bugs for the baby birds to eat. They stole a third of a bale of my pine straw to build their nests in the first place. But that was all okay. These mother birds are the workhorses and caregivers of the avian world.

But something disrupted their flow that year. You know what it was?

London. Our new dog.

London is a big dog, and dogs regularly need to do things in the yard. In our case, the side yard right out the door near where the birds would quietly build their nests. Now, the bird's tranquil habitat was the daily thoroughfare for our Goldendoodle. So whenever London came outside, the birds would get all agitated.

We particularly saw this agitation right when the baby birds needed to learn how to fly. It was time for those baby birds to jump out of the nest, but there was our big dog down below, and that caused considerable stress in the birds' lives. They were thinking, *Wait a minute. This is not what we'd planned. We have our territory. You have yours. Get that dog out of here.*

Even then, with the dog down below, the mother bird finally said to her babies, "It's time." And those baby birds came out of the nest. The mama was saying, "You can fly. You're ready to go forward. Off you go." And off they went. Sure enough, somewhere between the nest and the ground, those baby birds figured out how their wings worked. They started flapping like mad and flew off into the sky and it was like they were saying, "Hey, this is awesome! We're so glad we didn't stay in the nest."

This is a picture of our life in Christ. A nest is a good thing for a while. It's safe and comfortable and sheltered, and all our spiritual baby-needs are taken care of. But if we're not careful, then the giant of comfort tempts us to stay in the nest forever. Maybe we're worried about leaving the nest. We see a big dog below on the ground. We're not sure if we can fly or not. But staying in the nest is never our end goal. Comfort and familiarity are not what God points us toward. Jesus isn't in the business of flying to and fro for the rest of our lives, hand-delivering spiritual baby food to us.

Faith thrives in holy *discomfort*.

The calling of faith pushes us out of the nest. Jesus says, "Hey, you weren't made to live in the nest forever. You were made to live out in a broken world where there's conflict and risk." The gospel of Jesus pushes us out of the nest and says, "You're ready to fly. Off you go." Somewhere between the nest and the ground we figure out that our wings work. We see how Christ came into the world so he could send us out into the world. We see how we're filled with his Holy Spirit, and we can walk where Jesus walked and be the hands and feet of Jesus, and we say, "This flying is awesome. It's way better than the nest."

Jesus told a story about a successful man. That man had bumper crops and said to himself, "I'm going to build a bigger barn to hold all my banner crops. And then I'll have plenty to last me for a long while, so I'll just take things easy. I'll eat what I want, drink a little, and have a good time."

But, God said to the successful man, "You are a fool."

I don't know a lot, but I know you don't want to be called a fool by God!

God continued, "This is going to be your last day on earth and your soul is going to appear before God. What's more, you don't even know who will end up with all this stuff."

Rest assured, God is a generous God. He's not stingy. He doesn't need our stuff.

What God is doing is trying to help us see that there is a fight to be fought, a race to be run, something of eternal significance to be contended for. He's calling us to greater purpose, but he knows how easy it is to just eat a good meal, relax with a nice drink, and forget about the brevity of life on earth.

I'm talking about influence that God wants to give us. I'm talking about opportunities. I'm talking about walking in paths of righteousness for his name's sake. I'm talking about stepping out in obedience. I'm talking about prayer and action. If our hearts are wide open in faith, then God is wide open to us. If we take the risk and go where God invites us, then God's conduit is deep and wide. In faith, we're invited to enter into the story of a generous God. In faith, we're called to rally around the war cry that Christ has come and the battle is already won.

The Taunts End Today

In 1 Samuel 17, we see how comfort stymied the nation of Israel and David's three older brothers up at their army camp. They repeated their battle cry every day. They got suited up and went and stood on the front lines. They had God on their side and believed he was the one true God. But for forty days they were held back by comfort. They were prevented from moving forward by the lure of ease. The giant was calling the shots. He was dictating their lives. Goliath would come out every morning and evening and shake, rattle, and roar, and the Israelites would all say, "Nope, not today. Too dangerous. Too uncomfortable. Let's go have lunch. Let's stay in the tents where it's safe. If we run out of supplies someone will arrive with more. Maybe we'll do battle tomorrow."

We can act the same way today. We have our churches and our battle cries and there's an entire camp of us hanging out together in our comfort. But the giant is taunting us. We are failing to let the victory of Christ into our lives in the fullest way, because we aren't willing to step away from our sense of control, our ample supply, or our sense of material comfort. We won't accept a challenge and move out with God into whatever he is calling us to do. We shout our war cries, but we continue to shudder in the shadow of our giants.

The picture we tend to miss in the story of David and Goliath is that the little brother came on the scene and did in one day what his three older brothers and the whole army of Israel hadn't been able to do for a month and a half. Every day they'd been wavering. Every day their comfort held them back. Every day the giant kept coming and coming and coming. Then David showed up and said, "This is nuts. This is going to end today. What hasn't happened in the past forty days is going to happen in the next forty minutes."

It makes me wonder what God wants to do right here, right now, in our lives. Maybe we've been wavering. We've been waiting for a long time for all the pieces to line up before we can move. We want everything to get in place before some sort of good change happens. Instead, we just need to listen to God.

He's saying, *I am the God who can bring salvation today. Your giant is going down. In faith, you can step out of your comfort and go where I show you to go.* I bet all the pieces aren't going to line up for us at first. The whole pathway forward is not going to be revealed. The new direction God calls us in won't feel familiar and comfortable at first. Yet God says, *By my hand and by the might and the power of God, this victory is going to come.*

See, what matters is not that you and I wait until we feel fully strong. We don't need to learn how to fly before we jump out of the nest. What matters most is that we understand that we move in God's strength. As soon as we grasp that, we're ready for the battle. Sure, when we do that we could be put in an uncomfortable position. Yet we will also be in the place where we can see the salvation of God.

What does this look like? How can we make sure we don't lose God's opportunity by settling back into our comfort and complacency? Here are four truths to remember.

1. We remember that faith thrives in discomfort.

I spoke this message at our church, and when I came to this first point, it couldn't have gotten any quieter in the house. One of those "don't breathe" moments. Faith goes hand in hand with discomfort. *Oh, that's just great, Louie. Exactly what everybody wants to hear.*

But hey, don't let me get in between you and God's Word. Read the entire chapter of Hebrews 11, the "hall of fame" faith chapter in the Bible, and you'll see what I mean. "Faith is confidence in what we hope for and assurance about what we do not see" (v. 1). That's seldom comfortable.

In fact, the gospel is rooted in a place of discomfort—Christ's discomfort. The cross brought pain to Jesus in the same breath it brought freedom to us. We are alive because of Christ's discomfort. We can fully live because of the rugged cross. Christ endured what was uncomfortable so we could become the sons and daughters of God. This is our story. People ask, "What does it mean to be a Christian?" It means to put our faith in the work of Jesus. What is the work of Jesus? That he came to earth. He lived. He was crucified. He was resurrected. He ascended into heaven. He sent the Spirit of God, and he's now living inside of us. This is the gospel. This is what we believe, and it all hinges around a very uncomfortable moment.

Somehow as a people of God, if we're not careful, we can sing songs about the uncomfortable moment of Jesus while we live in the very comfortable moment of us. Thank you, Jesus—you took it all. But we forget what it truly means to identify with Christ. The Bible tells us that as Christ followers, we identify with his crucifixion just as much as we identify with his resurrection. Paul wrote in Galatians 2:20, "I have been crucified with Christ and I no longer live, but Christ lives in me. The life I now live in the body, I live by faith in the Son of God, who loved me and gave himself for me." That means our dreams and plans become merged with Christ's when we remember that death and life are both part of Christ's work. Romans 6:8 says, "Now if we died with Christ, we believe that we will also live with him." That's our call. To die with Christ and also to live with him.

Can you name anything in the life of faith that's completely comfortable? Resisting sin? Nope, not comfortable. Being transformed into the image of Christ? No, not comfortable either. Joining with Christ on his mission? No. Wondrous, but not always comfortable. That's why Paul says in 2 Corinthians 12:10, "For Christ's sake, I delight in weaknesses, in insults, in hardships, in persecutions, in difficulties. For when I am weak, then I am strong."

Faith thrives in holy discomfort. The greatest moments in life can often result from some of the most uncomfortable decisions being made. Nothing worth having comes without a cost.

A few months after my father passed away in 1995, Shelley and I were in a fog of discomfort. We had left a thriving ministry behind in Texas to help my mom with my father's care in Atlanta. But just before we relocated, a heart attack took him from us. We were confused, grieving death, between two cities and without jobs. The reason we were making the move vanished, leaving us in no-man's-land.

Not comfortable.

But in that tilled-up soil, a seed was planted, a seed we have watched grow and blossom into all things Passion. God needed us open-handed, flexible, and available so faith could give birth to something new and bold and beautiful.

2. We remember the point of our lives is the fame of Jesus.

How can we make sure we don't lose God's opportunity by settling back in our comfort and complacency? We remember the point of our lives is the fame of Jesus.

If our only motivation for taking down a giant is our freedom, then we won't have all the motivation that's needed. God's glory is also the motivation for us to walk in victory over the giants in our lives. Our freedom and God's glory are forever intertwined, and if we forget about the glory of God, then we won't be willing to pay the price of whatever step it is that God's asking us to take. When we see the glory of God, we'll understand that there is no cost too great to pay to make his name known in our life.

The army of Israel was complacent in their comfort. They had food. They had tents. They had a war cry. They had armor. They had little brothers who would replenish their supply.

But they weren't moving.

David showed up and said, "Hey, Goliath, you're insulting my God. That's got to stop right now. It stops because you're dishonoring my God. This is the God I worship, the God I commune with, the God who loves me, the God I've been hanging out with for years in the shepherd's field. And you are taking glory away from the name of the one true God of all gods. That needs to stop immediately."

Philippians 2 is an amazing passage. Paul talks about how he wants us to give our lives away for one another. The point of life is not to think about me and mine, but to think about you and yours. Not to get my stuff in order, but to think about what I can do to help you. Paul gives us a picture of that in verse 5: "You must have the same attitude that Christ Jesus had" (NLT).

Jesus had the full rights and full nature and essence of God, yet he stepped out of heaven and came to earth. He humbled himself and became a man. He took the nature of a servant. Jesus obeyed God the Father and went to the cross. Because of all that, the Bible says, God "exalted him to the highest place and gave him the name that is above every name, that at the name of Jesus every knee should bow, in heaven and on earth and under the earth, and every tongue acknowledge that Jesus Christ is Lord, to the glory of God the Father" (Philippians 2:9–11).

Why did Jesus ultimately take this step? For our well-being? No. For the glory of God. Why did Jesus empty himself? Because he loved us? No. It was ultimately for the glory of God. Of course God loves us. Of course God cares about us. The love of Jesus shines a light on God. And our response is to live for his glory.

3. We align ourselves with God.

How can we make sure we don't lose God's opportunity by settling back in our comfort and complacency? We align ourselves with God.

Any of us can sit back and decide it's easier to follow the world's message. A point of view. The example of someone else's life. Someone else's standard for material wealth. Ultimately, we can rationalize anything we want. But the invitation for each of us is not to come and follow our neighbor or fellow believer. It's to follow Christ.

Purposeful, meaningful, lasting life is the by-product of walking closely with the Father, Son, and Spirit. When Jesus was a boy, he asked, "Didn't you know I must be about my Father's business?" (Luke 2:49, author's paraphrase). When the Spirit fell on the early followers of Jesus in the book of Acts, his power propelled them into the world to proclaim the grace and goodness of the gospel at all cost.

God doesn't call us to avoid the danger of a lost and dying world. Rather, he leads us into it with the sword of the Spirit in our hands. He says, "We must quickly carry out the tasks assigned us by the one who sent us. The night is coming, and then no one can work" (John 9:4 NLT).

My friend Andy Stanley reminds us that we don't end up where we hope to end up. Our lives ultimately end up wherever our path is headed right now. So we have to be diligent about who and what we align ourselves with. Because whatever (or whomever) we saddle up with is going to determine where we arrive months and years from now.

Who are you linking your life to? Who helps you decide

what you spend, where you go, what you watch, what ranks at the top of your to-do list?

To walk with Christ is to imitate him. To imitate Christ is to live with ultimate purpose.

4. We remember life is short.

How can we make sure we don't lose God's opportunity by settling back into our comfort and complacency? We remember that life is short. It's a mission statement for all of us to ingest into our hearts and lives. "Life is short." We forget this so easily. But it's so important.

When David's three older brothers and all the rest of the army of Israel got to the end of their days, I believe they all shared a big regret. They'd wasted forty days sitting on that hillside. Forty days they would never get back. Hey, life is short, and what a waste to spend forty days under the influence of a taunting giant. They had the power of God with them. They could have moved forward if they'd wanted to. But they didn't. They chose comfort instead of discomfort. They chose to waste their days rather than claim their days.

What's the danger for us? It's that we do the same thing. We waste our days thinking, *I've got time. I'll obey God in the next season of life. I'll obey God when I get enough money in the bank. I'll obey God when my kids are out of the house. I'll obey God when I'm older. I'll obey God when I'm finished having fun. I'll obey God after I'm married. I'll obey God when my marriage gets easier. I'll obey God when it seems like it's a more logical time to take the next step.*

But God is breaking into our story today. He says, *The battle is already won. I want you to step out with me right now, today. Don't delay. Life is short. Don't waste your days.*

We might live to be eighty-five or ninety years old, but in the end it's all pretty much the same. God gives us breath. And then our days are gone. Quickly, a match is lit. Quickly, a match is extinguished. *Poof.* Wow, that went by fast. If the Enemy can keep us good and comfortable, then he can prompt us to waste our days. But we are not a people of comfort. We are a people of faith.

To be clear, complacency is not about what we own or don't own. It's cultivating and tolerating an off-target heart. Complacency springs from the root of *me* that says we should protect what we have because we earned it—and we deserve more. That kind of thinking results from having our eyes glued to the wrong world. Namely, this passing world, instead of the one that's coming.

The reminder of God is that we rally around the cross. We don't have time to waste our days. Yes, we rest in the work of Jesus. Yes, his yoke is easy and our burden is light. But yes, we work with all our might. Paul says in 1 Corinthians 9:26, "I do not run like someone running aimlessly; I do not fight like a boxer beating the air." We live on a planet with billions and billions of people who've never heard of Jesus. That's why time is short. This world is rattling at the hinges, and we have the answer. We have the hope. We have the truth. We have the life. We have Jesus.

That's what matters—letting Jesus be known. The goal of our faith isn't to settle into a nice comfortable job and a nice easy routine. The goal is to say, "God, I'm available for whatever you want me to do. When you call on me I will step forward and say, 'In the name of the Lord God Almighty, I will step into the fight.' Not in my ability. Not in my power. Not in my strength. But in the name of Jesus. Life is short, and I don't have enough time to have a complacent heart."

Life Is Short. God Is Big.

Maybe that last point scared you a bit. "Life is short." Maybe you feel like you've wasted too much time already. You have spent your full forty days (and then some) in your tent being taunted by your giant. You want to reclaim those days but you don't know how to begin. There's great encouragement for us all here in these words. Life is short, yes. But *God is big.* God is able to redeem every situation. He is able to breathe new life into every heart. God is able to restore anything that's been lost or broken or stolen. He is able to do "far more than we dare ask or imagine" (Ephesians 3:21 CEV).

Really, the combination of both of those two small phrases becomes our mission statement for living by faith. (1) *Life is short.* And (2) *God is big.* Repeat those two small phrases if you need to. They're huge in meaning and weight. Let them roll through your mind and heart. *Life is short. God is big. Life is short. God is big. Life is short. God is big.* Do you hear that voice?

It's the voice of the giant slayer.

It's the voice of the disciple maker.

It's the voice of the martyr who pays the ultimate price for the sake of the gospel.

It's the voice of the movement starter who sees what can be and takes a risk.

It's the voice of the church planter who could choose a more comfortable way.

It's the voice of those who impact culture in Jesus' name.

It's the voice of the prayer warrior.

It's the voice of the injustice fighter who has been moved by Christ's freedom and is compelled to free others.

It's the voice of the compassionate one who sells his stuff to provide for the less fortunate.

It's the voice of the teacher who pours into students everything she can.

It's the voice of those who are salt and light in the entertainment industry, even when it's not the most rewarded choice.

It's the voice of the chaplain who cares for the dying with hope and dignity and the gospel.

It's the voice of the psychologist and the doctor and the surgeon who reflect Christ in all they do.

It's the voice of the recovery counselor who refuses to quit.

It's the voice of the youth pastor and the senior pastor and the associate pastor and the lead pastor and the teaching pastor and the missions pastor and the administrative pastor and the children's pastor and the men's pastor and the women's pastor who live well, love truth, and care for people.

It's the voice of the artist and the dancer who promote something and someone above themselves.

It's the voice of the business leader who refuses to take all the profits.

It's the voice of the blue-collar worker who does his job as an act of worship.

It's the voice of the technology worker who lives by the Spirit.

It's the voice of the mother and father who shepherd their kids in a way that inspires them to leave the nest.

It's the voice of the grandmother and the grandfather who set a godly example or obedience throughout every season.

It's the voice of the one who speaks to his neighbor about the big things in life.

It's the voice of anyone who holds doors open that help others get to Jesus.

It's the voice of those who are on the front lines right now pushing through the darkness and saying, "We're going to bring the gospel of Jesus to people no matter what the cost."

This is the nature of what it means to follow Jesus.

Let these two small phrases roll through your mind and heart. *Life is short. God is big. Life is short. God is big. Life is short. God is big.* Do you hear that voice? Oh, I pray you hear that voice. We begin to listen by worshipping God. When we breathe in worship, we know and feel that life is short and God is big. Our hearts are emboldened. We are ready to move into action. Complacency leads to inaction, but worship moves us into action. It puts holy urgency in our lives.

I have a deep conviction that the greatest regret any of us will ever know is that of standing before Jesus knowing we lived too safe, too comfortable, too short-sighted. Realizing we were gluttons for pleasure when we were supposed to be lean warriors for others' freedom and Jesus' fame.

Just imagine if David's three older brothers and the army of Israel had felt such a holy urgency. They wouldn't have settled for forty days of comfort and taunting. They would have been making plans and moving forward in the name of God. I can just picture them. One soldier would say, "You know, this giant needs to go down today. We're not listening to him one moment longer. I know he's tall, but here's the plan. I'll charge his feet. I'll twist his toenails. As soon as he falls over, I'll stab him in the throat." And another soldier would say, "Yeah. I was thinking of a similar strategy. I know this giant looks intimidating, but we can do it. I'll take a spear and throw it straight through his left eye. When he goes down I'll sit on his head and suffocate him. This giant is going down." They would refuse to waste forty more days of their lives. They would do what God called them to do on the battlefield.

We fight complacency whenever we ask God to help us see what hangs in the balance. Faith is never just about us and our lives. Faith is about benefiting people we don't even know. Not only is our freedom, our salvation, our purpose in life, our getting on board with what God has for us hanging in the balance, but other people's lives and freedom are at stake too. God has a plan to move us out to help other people. It's all done for his glory and fame. We have the ability to do what Christ wants us to do. "For we are God's handiwork, created in Christ Jesus to do good works, which God prepared in advance for us to do" (Ephesians 2:10).

After David killed Goliath, the entire army of Israel benefited—not to mention every man, woman, and child in the entire nation of Israel. When the Philistines saw that their champion was dead, the whole army of Israel pursued them. Israel threw off the yoke of the Philistines. They pursued them and took their wealth. A whole nation was made free because of the faith of one person.

There might be a nation waiting on you today. There might be a whole family waiting on you today. There might be a whole classroom of children waiting on you today. There may be a whole group of people waiting for deliverance because you're stuck in complacency. God will accomplish his plans one way or another, yet God is inviting you to be part of his plans. It won't always be comfortable. It won't always be easy. You will probably need to step forward, not knowing anything other than you're far out with God on the end of the limb, believing that he wants to make his fame known to this generation of people. Yet if you move in faith, God will always breathe life on your journey.

I think that's the way the shepherd boy was thinking when he walked into the Valley of Elah.

Your Giant
Is Dead

A chilly morning wind sliced through the tense valley air. The clanking of cooking pots heard throughout the war camp suddenly stopped. Every head in the Israelite camp turned. Every eye fixed on the incredulous sight that approached the valley floor.

One young man walked toward the giant.

On the other side of the valley, Goliath couldn't believe it either. Squinting, he shaded his brow and stared toward the lone figure that dared challenge him. "Who does this guy think he is?" Goliath muttered. "Someone actually wants to fight me?" He motioned to his armor bearer, gripped a javelin, and started to march forward. The giant was eager. Unafraid.

For forty days Goliath's vicious taunts had echoed through the valley. Everyone in the Israelite camp had heard the taunts every day. "YOU COWARDS! Someone stand up and fight me, or are all you too afraid? You're worthless! The whole lot of you. Powerless. Weak. Just like your God. I defy you, and I defy your God!"

The taunts had stopped every one of the Israelites in their tracks. For forty straight days, they'd been frozen in fear. The Israelites hated the giant, but they couldn't seem to stop the taunts of his voice either.

At nine feet tall and undefeated, Goliath was known throughout the land as a savage killer. Soldiers had seen him rip into his enemies, mauling them, leaving them bloody, desperate, destroyed, and dead. He was impenetrable. Undefeatable. No one had answered the call to fight him. And no one knew that better than the giant himself.

But now . . . one small frame dared approach.

"He's not even wearing armor," one of Israel's fighters said. "We've never seen this soldier before. Get him out of there before he gets hurt."

But no one ran to the boy's aid.

Goliath spat on the ground in disgust. Shrugging back his shoulders as if awakened to battle, he adjusted his heavy armor. He could see that his opponent was only a boy. The giant continued to march. He drew his arm back and it grew taut as he aimed his javelin.

Goliath's accuracy was deadly. All it would take was one throw and the young man would lie breathless.

The armies on both hills erupted in shouts at the impending fight. The Israelites yelled for the kid to come back. The Philistines roared, "Kill him! Rip his head off!"

Goliath wanted to get in a few jeers of his own. Still on the march, he bellowed with jest and anger, "Am I a dog that you would come against me with sticks? Come here, and I'll feed your bones to the beasts of the earth!"

Unfazed, David focused on the task ahead. The boy appeared weaponless except for a rod and staff in one hand and a sling in the other. His eyes measured the landscape. He instinctively gauged the wind speed, the trajectory of flight, the gap between himself and the giant.

This was no ordinary boy standing before the Philistine champion. He had been summoned from the fields and anointed as the future king of Israel. He was in a line of royalty. The Spirit of the Lord had come upon the young David in power and might.

And David was more than tough. Fueling his confidence was an unusually close relationship with God. God wasn't some faraway idea to David. The boy knew God was much more than the God of his ancestors. As the boy spent long nights watching over the sheep, he sang worship songs to God. He loved God and knew that God loved him. And David was convinced that his God—not the idols of the Philistines—was the one true and living God. *David loved God, and he knew that God loved him.*

"Listen to me, you uncircumcised Philistine," David shouted. "You come at me with a sword and spear and javelin, but I come against you in the name of the Lord Almighty, my Father, the God of the armies of Israel. This is the God you have defied. My Father will hand you over to me today, and I'm going to strike you down and cut off your head! I'm going to feed your whole army to the birds of the air and the beasts of the field!"

No one on either side of the valley could believe what he heard. The soldiers wondered if the kid was crazy. Maybe he had a death wish.

But David called louder still, "Do you hear me? When I'm finished with you, the whole world will know our God is God!"

Goliath snorted and stamped his foot like a bull. He charged toward David, and the gap between the fighters narrowed. Fifty yards. Forty. Thirty.

David reached into his bag of stones and loaded his sling with a smooth, round rock. He ran forward a few quick steps while looping his sling in a circular motion. He searched for the exact spot he needed to hit. The giant was covered from head to toe in armor. Only one tiny, narrow, bare patch of skin lay vulnerable. A needle in a haystack. A bull's-eye in the wind.

Twenty-five yards. Twenty.

With all his might, Goliath prepared to hurl his javelin toward the boy. The javelin would speed toward his foe, deadly in its intent. But before Goliath could act, David aimed his sling and let go. His rock flew steady and sure up toward the giant.

Smack!

The stone hit the giant's forehead and sunk in. Right between his eyes. The rock landed with such force it stopped the giant in his tracks.

Stunned, Goliath swayed. He gave a little shake, righted himself, and tried to step forward. It was no use. His eyes rolled back into his head. Out on his feet, his body toppled and crashed into the dirt with a *thud* that reverberated through the valley. Facedown, Goliath lay motionless. He was already dead.

The Philistines fell silent. The Israelites blinked in disbelief.

Throughout the Valley of Elah, it felt like time stood still.

David didn't want any questions to remain. He

sprinted up to Goliath and grabbed the giant's sword from his sheath. Using both hands, he lifted the weapon as high as he could and swung it downward against Goliath's neck.

Bam!

The head rolled free. The giant's campaign of terror was dead and done. As if on cue, the Philistine army turned tail and ran for their lives.

Simultaneously, a horn sounded from the Israelite camp. *"Charge!"* An emboldened Israel surged forward, swords and spears in hand, and pursued their enemies with newfound furor.

"It's over," they shouted as they pumped their fists in the air. "The giant is finished. We win!"

CHAPTER 6

Anger Must Fall

—

Ask someone if he or she is an angry person, and most will deny it at first.

"I don't go around in a rage every day," they'll say. "I don't yell at the people I work with. I don't lash out at my wife or throw things around the house."

But dig under the top layer of our lives just a bit, and it can be a different story. Sometimes the anger emerges overtly. Sometimes the anger is there, but it isn't seen for a long, long time. The anger lurks underneath the surface, waiting for the right spark to set it off. Here's what that can look like.

Our team used to work out of a one-hundred-year-old house about an hour north of Atlanta in a sprawling suburb. The house sat on Main Street and was classic yesteryear, with a wide front porch and a helter-skelter floor plan due to multiple add-ons over time.

One day after a huge event our team had hosted in another

state, we gathered for a staff meeting in one of the downstairs rooms, reflecting on all we had just experienced. When the meeting ended a lot of us headed out to go to lunch together. As I stepped outside I remembered I'd left my wallet on my desk upstairs, so while others piled into nearby cars I bounded up the back stairway and down the hall into my office.

My office space was an expanded attic-like area with windows on three sides. The room had a pitched roof of pine slats and was situated near the front of the house above the porch. To get into my main office you stepped up and walked through an odd-shaped room I used as a small library. Just as I jetted through that little space, I was sure I smelled something burning. I wheeled around in the bigger room and passed through again.

Sure enough, something smelled of trouble—that acrid odor that lets you know something's burning that's not supposed to be on fire. I looked in every direction. No flames. No smoke. I opened a panel that led to a crawl space that contained a heating unit. No smell there either. I walked back into the big room. Nothing. Back in the little passageway, I definitely smelled something burning. But what? Where?

By now everyone was waiting. *Classic Louie. Forgot something, now can't find it.*

Perplexed, I walked back into my main office and paused, scanning the room for any sign of danger. Then I saw it. Smoke! On the far wall was a recessed nook with two long shelves. On the top shelf sat an award I'd received years ago. It looked like an Oscar and had smoke coming from its head. Yep! Circles of gray smoke, almost like rings, puffed from within and rose above the statue. Weird. I knew I was close to finding the source of the fire. I put my hand on the wall and it felt warm, so I did what I'd seen on television. I knelt down and felt the carpeted floor. *HOT.* That's all I needed to know!

I ran back downstairs and calmly said, "The house is on fire, everybody. Get your stuff out while you can."

A few minutes passed before fire trucks were outside and firemen were imploring me to get out of my office. I kept trying to help, pointing them to the spot on the wall and floor where the action was. Soon their thermal-imaging equipment confirmed that there was, in fact, a hot spot between the wall and the exterior of the house. Just like that, they ripped out the carpet and the floor and the entire wall. Bits and pieces of our house were now coming through the front window and another one up the middle stairs.

We were going to miss lunch.

Fortunately, I'd forgotten my wallet that day, and as a result the whole house was probably spared. Once the dust had settled, I was allowed back into my office to get a few things. The fire was fairly contained to one spot in the subflooring. Other than a mess, things were going to be fine.

I asked what the cause of the fire was. A fireman shined his light on a spot where an electrical wire had become frayed. The outer covering was gone, exposing the current-filled wire to plywood. The problem had been shoddy work, years ago. When this room had been added, someone had cut a corner. Instead of drilling through the floor joist (the long beam that supports the flooring) and feeding the wire through it, they'd just looped the wire over the joist and let it ride under the plywood flooring. Over time (lots of time) as the house had shifted, the wire rubbed against the joist, eventually sparking into a flame. I asked the fireman how long it has been smoldering under there before it caught fire.

"Hard to say," he said, "but from the looks of it, a week to ten days. Maybe longer."

What?! While we'd been away hosting one of the biggest events in our history, our entire office had been simmering, ready to burst into flames at any minute.

That's usually how the giant of anger works in our lives. We say, on the surface, everything's fine. "I don't consider myself the angry type," we tell our friends. But underneath the subfloor of our heart something's been rubbing us the wrong way for a while. Unchecked and unresolved, we are headed for trouble. That's why dealing with the giant of rejection is so important for us. Most anger is rooted in some form of rejection. Something that was or wasn't said. Something that was repeatedly done to us. Something we deserved but were deprived of. A hurt. A wound. A stab.

What do we do about the giant of anger?

Anger Days

For me, it doesn't take long to pinpoint an area of my life where there's been friction. It's bike riding. I have a road bicycle, and my idea of a great Saturday afternoon off is to go for a long, sweaty ride. I love the physicality of the workouts. I do a lot of great thinking and praying while I'm alone on a bike.

But here's the problem. Bike riders and car drivers aren't known for getting along—and car drivers own the road. Drivers don't like the idea that some dude is out here in their lane slowing down the process of getting to their destination—especially on the country roads I like to ride on most. It's an environment where anger can flare on both sides.

I've been caught in this clash before. Just the other day I was riding along, minding my own business, when a car passed me, then quickly turned to the right without checking to see how close he was to me. If I hadn't slammed on my brakes, I'd have plowed straight into him. I wasn't happy about that. In fact, I was pretty angry. My safety had been threatened. It was a gut-check type of response. I shook my fist at the driver and started yelling at the top of my lungs for him to turn around and come back. What was I going to do if he did? Fight him? Fortunately, he kept going. In a cooler moment, I wondered what I'd done. Me shaking my fist was the reaction that could be seen. That was the smell of smoke in the old house. But I needed to ask myself: What was lurking below that made me lash out this way?

Anger is not wrong. But if anger is uncontrolled, stuffed, misplaced, or given full vent, then anger can do us a lot of harm. Scripture is clear that anger is a giant that can shut down God's possibility for our lives. If we're not careful, our anger will burn somebody else's life down. We can also count on this: unchecked anger is definitely going to burn our lives down too.

I stress again that anger isn't always wrong in and of itself. Ephesians 4:26 says, "In your anger do not sin." And James 1:19 says, "Everyone should be quick to listen, slow to speak and slow to become angry." Jesus himself felt anger. He acted on this powerful emotion yet never sinned. He had strong words for his disciples on several occasions. He threw the money changers out of the temple. He once walked into a dinner party and immediately began insulting the host (see Luke 11:37–53). So Scripture shows that there's a time to be angry and a time to rightly express our anger. But that's not what we're talking about in this chapter, because there're a lot of ways that anger works its way into our lives where it becomes a problem. That's what we want to address: when anger becomes a giant. Have you ever experienced anything like this?

- *Wrongly felt anger.* You feel angry about something that never happened. You thought somebody did or said or felt something bad. But the people didn't really do or say or feel that way. The anger is wrongly felt—and sometimes wrongly acted upon too—but it's real anger in your life, to be sure.

- *Rightly felt anger that's wrongly expressed.* You genuinely have something to be angry about, but the way you're expressing your anger comes out all manner of wrong ways. Your anger blows up bridges. It damages the people around you, and it damages you too.

- *Rightly felt anger that's never expressed.* You're angry, but you pretend everything's fine. You stuff your anger. You never speak about it. You never address the truth of your feelings. Repressing anger can be one of the most destructive things you can do. It poses a huge health risk. Not to mention you're living a lie.

There are a million reasons why people are angry today, so please don't let me shrink yours down to a simple phrase. People can be angry at their parents. People can be angry toward spouses (or ex-spouses). Toward bosses. Toward a lousy job. Toward second-grade teachers who told them they wouldn't amount to anything. Toward neighbors who play their music too loud. Toward a political party or ideology they don't agree with. Toward their children who aren't living up to their expectations. Anger can happen anytime we feel betrayed. We feel overlooked. We feel slighted. We feel belittled. We wanted something, or we hoped for something, and we didn't get what we wanted. Now we're angry.

How about you? Take some time to take a short self-inventory of your life. As you work through the list below, does anything stick out at you in the sense that it's made you angry? Circle the ones that bear the most weight in your life. I've used "parent" a lot in the list, but you can put someone else in the story. A friend. A coworker. A boss. A grandparent. An ex-boyfriend or girlfriend. A brother or sister. A coach. A teacher. A pastor. An industry. An institution. A country. A government. A terrorist. The circumstances of life. God. You feel betrayed or belittled or cheated. You wanted something but didn't get it.

Circle as many as apply.

Someone abandoned me.

Someone wasn't interested in me.

Someone picked somebody or something else over me.

Someone abused me.

Somebody I cared about was emotionally unavailable to me.

My parent left my family.

My dad/mom cheated on us. He/she didn't just cheat on my other parent, he/she cheated on all of us.

My parent lives with another family.

I'm angry because someone else's kids get my parent's attention every day.

I'm angry because my dad or mom is too busy for me.

I'm angry with my dad or mom because he/she didn't take care of us.

I'm angry with my dad or mom because he/she didn't take care of himself/herself.

I'm angry with a parent because he/she won't face the facts.

My dad/mom is too aggressive/too passive.

My dad/mom embarrasses me.

My dad/mom is gone all the time.

I'm angry at my parent's boss because my parent was let go.

I'm angry at another company because they hurt the business of my parent's company.

I'm angry at the man/woman who stole my dad/mom from us.

I'm angry at the kids who are with my dad/mom right now.

I'm angry at the place where my dad/mom works too much.

I'm mad at the doctor for not saving my dad/mom.

I'm angry with God because my loved one died in that accident.

I'm angry because I didn't get to say goodbye.

I'm angry with my son/daughter for ignoring the truth and wasting his/her life.

I'm angry with my family for giving all the attention to my problem sibling.

I'm mad at my mom/dad for putting so much stress on my dad/mom.

I'm mad at my mom for nagging my dad.

I'm angry at my dad for ignoring my mom.

I'm angry at God for not stopping a person I love from hurting himself.

I'm angry because of all the hurtful things a person has called me.

I'm angry because of all the things a person has said to me.

I'm angry because of all the things a person never said to me.

I'm angry because my parent was never a spiritual leader for me.

I'm angry because my mom or dad never even wanted me.

I'm angry because I was never good enough for my parent.

I'm angry because _____.

You might be angry at God. You might be angry at life. Some of you are just angry at everything and everybody. Maybe you circled everything on the list. It's amazing how harmful anger can be when it comes on the scene. The good news is that God in heaven has killed the giants in our lives. Jesus Christ Almighty, in his life, death, burial, and resurrection, has killed the giant called anger. The giant of anger is dead. It may still be talking to you and me, it might still be taunting us, it may still have deadly venom in its fangs, but the giant of anger is already dead.

Shaky Territory

In the story of David and Goliath, I don't see David being all that angry. Maybe he was righteously angry because God was being taunted and nobody was doing anything about it. That's the right kind of anger. What I see, though, is David being surrounded by some angry people who weren't righteously angry. Particularly

David's older brother Eliab, whom we've already talked about a bit. In 1 Samuel 17, when the young shepherd boy David came up to the battle lines, he heard Goliath taunting the Israelites, asked some questions, and moved into action. But when David's older brother Eliab heard about the plan, the Bible says he "burned with anger at him" (v. 28).

Think this through with me. Eliab already knew David was a special kid. Eliab already had seen God's favor on David's life. David already had been anointed king. He'd already killed the lion and the bear. He already was a fantastic musician and song-writer. He did just fine taking care of their father's sheep, an important source of provision and income for the family. And in light of all that, when David came up to the battle, Eliab should have been supportive of David. But instead, Eliab's heart raged with anger. That was wrongly expressed anger and undoubtedly wrongly felt. Eliab might have felt slighted in the family, but he didn't have a good reason to be mad at David. Eliab was dealing with his own problems. His feelings were rooted in his inability to process life under the canopy of the grace and the love of God. Here's how Eliab expressed his anger—verbally.

Note 1 Samuel 17:28. Eliab looked at David and asked him, "Why have you come down here? And with whom did you leave those few sheep in the wilderness? I know how conceited you are and how wicked your heart is; you came down only to watch the battle." Can you hear the accusatory tone in Eliab's voice? Eliab was reframing David in his own opinion. Eliab was belittling his brother. Look between the lines. Eliab was saying, "I am a fighting man. I am the head of the brothers. You tend sheep. (And just a few sheep, by the way.) Did you have to hire a little sheep herder to take care of your little sheep while you came up here where the big boys are today?" This is what angry people do. They find a way to knock down the people around them. At the end of the verse, Eliab called David "conceited" and announced that David's heart was "wicked." This was questionable territory for Eliab. Anytime we start making accusations about another person's heart, we are on shaky ground. We don't know what is in another person's heart; only God knows that. When people make character assassinations about other people, they're typically tipping their hand at what's going on in their own heart.

Maybe you think I'm reading into the text too much. But we saw this earlier when the prophet Samuel first came to anoint David. Jesse, the father of all of the boys, paraded his sons out one by one for the prophet to take a look at. Eliab, the oldest, tallest, and toughest son, was led out first. "But the LORD said to Samuel, 'Do not consider his appearance or his height, for I have rejected him. The LORD does not look at the things people look at. People look at the outward appearance, but the LORD looks at the heart'" (1 Samuel 16:7).

That's where a seed of anger was planted in Eliab's heart. He could have trusted the wisdom of the Lord. God knew best who should become the next king. God knew Eliab wouldn't make a good king. Eliab could have trusted that. Instead, Eliab went the other way and poured fertilizer on that seed. He nurtured the seed of anger. Watered it and tended it and let it grow and bloom. Eliab wasn't picked, and not getting picked can be one of the huge roots of anger in our lives. Eliab felt slighted. He burned with jealousy. He wanted the same honors David had. If only Eliab would have opened his heart to the Lord, the Lord would have done a work in him. But Eliab chose to go the other way and stoke the furnace of his anger. Jealousy is a tough thing to carry because it causes us to compare and compete. It silences us from celebrating and affirming. When we live in families that compare and compete, but can't celebrate and affirm, we live at war. It's because the giant of anger has stood in the middle of the battlefield, yelled out his taunts to us, and taken a foothold in our hearts.

One of the positive examples given to us in the story of David and Goliath is that David didn't let the anger of Eliab slow him down. David went on and killed Goliath. David freed his people, and he took the oppressive yoke off his brothers and all the nation of Israel. David continued forward in the power of God's name and did what God called him to do. Eliab could have done that too. He wasn't going to be king, but he could have been a lot more than he was. Eliab could have been David's champion from the start.

The happy ending in Eliab's life is mentioned later on in a different book in the Bible. In 1 Chronicles 12:9, years after Goliath was killed, Eliab was given the position of third-in-charge of King David's army. Eliab was musical, just like his younger brother, and Eliab went on to become a musician in David's army (1 Chronicles 15:20). And finally, in 1 Chronicles 27:18 (although he's called "Elihu" here), it says that Eliab, a brother of David, was eventually made the leader over the whole tribe of Judah. So I like to think that Eliab and David eventually buried the hatchet. The Lord worked in Eliab's heart, and his ways were changed. He stopped being angry and jealous, and King David rewarded his brother with a significant position of leadership in his kingdom. There was just all that mess of anger in the meantime that Eliab needed to deal with.

Five Smooth Stones of Truth

Maybe you're looking for an instant fix to your anger. You want to be changed overnight. But a real and lasting fix seldom arrives instantaneously. God morphs our life little by little, bit by bit.

Goliath taunted the Israelites every morning and night. The Devil prowls around continually and wants to devour us every day. The key to real, lasting change in our spiritual life is consistently filling ourselves up with faith. Giants seldom go away quickly. Our invitation is to continually remind ourselves that Jesus has already won. We continually need to link up to what he has done and who he is in us. Then we talk to ourselves like God talks to us. We tell ourselves biblical truths. When we do these

We believe
what God
did for us
is *greater*
than what
anyone could
do against us.

things and align ourselves with the plans of God, then little by little things change. We replace anger with reading God's Word. We replace the angry conversations in our minds with praying for the people we're angry at. We begin to see others through Jesus' eyes. We invite Christ to have the full rule and reign in our hearts.

What follows are five smooth stones of truth we can throw at the giant of anger. Jesus has already done the real work, and the giant has already fallen. But as we've discussed, ridding ourselves of giants is both a now-and-not-yet reality. The battle is over, yes. But the struggle continues. By God's grace, he has won the victory for us, and he will win the victory for us, day by day by day.

How is anger dealt with? How does this giant fall? When we throw the following five smooth stones of truth.

1. We remind ourselves we aren't perfect to begin with.

When we are angry at someone else, we must understand that Someone has already been angry at us. This can be a tricky thing to grasp, because the "Someone" is God, and we don't like to think of God as angry. We misunderstand the wrath of God. When we think of God's "wrath" we tend to overlay it with our understanding of human wrath. We picture someone strutting around a room, shaking his fist, throwing things at the wall. That's how we picture wrath. But God's wrath and human wrath aren't the same thing.

The Bible indicates that God does indeed hold out wrath toward people who don't know him and toward sin in the lives of believers. God is both loving and wrathful at the same time. He is wrathful because he is righteous. He is wrathful because he is holy. The things we tolerate, he doesn't tolerate. The small sins we let creep into our lives, he does not let creep into his. His righteousness burns like a flame of glory. His wrath is the eternal flame of the holiness and the perfection of God. Really, God's "wrath" just means that he exists. God walks into the equation of human life with its sin, and a holy God exists with the fire of righteousness and supremacy. God's wrath means he can't have anything to do with sin.

J. I. Packer goes to the dictionary and writes,

> *Wrath* is an old English word defined in my dictionary as "deep, intense anger and indignation." *Anger* is defined as "stirring of resentful displeasure and strong antagonism, by a sense of injury or insult"; *indignation* as "righteous anger aroused by injustice and baseness." Such is wrath. And wrath, the Bible tells us, is an attribute of God.[1]

It's important to grasp this, so we need to keep a new picture in mind. God's wrath doesn't mean he is out of control and pitching a fit. His wrath is much more a "positional" wrath than a "raging" wrath. It's a character-driven refusal to have anything to do with that which is unholy. God, by nature of being a holy

God, must turn away from sin. Yes, he's a God of wrath, but he is not a God of outrage. Yes, there's still a fierce anger on behalf of God that we need to contend with. It's an intense anger, a severe anger, an anger where there is no gray area. Yet it's always a positional anger of God's righteous character refusing to be associated with sin.

Paul describes it like this: "But because of your stubbornness and your unrepentant heart, you are storing up wrath against yourself for the day of God's wrath, when his righteous judgment will be revealed" (Romans 2:5).

So let's use this biblical definition of God's wrath—a righteous wrath—and clothe ourselves in the truth of this extended definition. Although God's wrath is not human wrath, it's still a very serious wrath. Using the biblical definition of God's wrath, we are reminded that long before anyone ever betrayed or belittled us, we betrayed and belittled God. And we were forgiven! So the person who has been forgiven much has much room to forgive others.

That helps us put our anger into perspective.

When I'm angry because I haven't received respect or if I feel belittled or betrayed, then I can remind myself of the fire of God's wrath. In my sin I have betrayed God. Yet God forgave me. So I can forgive others.

Psalm 85 is so strong here. Notice the first few verses. The psalmist couldn't even go very far without saying, "We've just got to stop right here." That's what *Selah* means.

You, LORD, showed favor to your land;
  you restored the fortunes of Jacob.
You forgave the iniquity of your people
  and covered all their sins. [Selah.]
You set aside all your wrath
  and turned from your fierce anger.
Restore us again, God our Savior,
  and put away your displeasure toward us.
Will you be angry with us forever?
  Will you prolong your anger through all
    generations?
Will you not revive us again,
  that your people may rejoice in you?
Show us your unfailing love, LORD,
  and grant us your salvation. (vv. 1–7)

That's the perspective we need to keep in mind. God has already forgiven much in our lives. That helps to keep us humble. That helps us stay off our high horse of moral superiority. That helps us forgive others.

2. We remind ourselves that God has made peace with us.

The second stone of truth is closely aligned with the first. God has always loved us, but he hated our sin and he hated our choices. He had an anger burning toward the way we treated him. Yet God has made peace with us. That's the second stone. A reminder of this truth.

Isaiah the prophet called Jesus the "Prince of Peace" (Isaiah 9:6). This is good news for an angry world. Jesus Christ is in the world and he's over and around and within the world, and he comes as a Wonderful Counselor and the Prince of Peace. Jesus is coming to the negotiating table and saying, "I have authority from heaven to broker a peace treaty. I have all authority to sit at the table and talk about your wrongs, but I'm not going to do that. I'm here to offer you a deal, to offer you peace, to offer you what no one else can offer you: salvation."

In Ephesians 2:11–18, Paul describes Jesus as "our peace." Jesus comes before God the Father and makes peace for us. How does Jesus do that? He does it through his shed blood poured out on the cross.

Whenever we're angry, we can rally back around the cross. That's why I keep talking about the cross. That's why we sing about the cross at church. That's why we celebrate the cross. That's why we don't move away from the cross, because it was at the cross where God, in his holy anger, made peace with us. That's tremendous news for us! God isn't angry with us anymore. Why? Because all of the righteous anger and holy wrath of God landed on Jesus at the cross. God's anger has been satisfied. We run to Jesus and find a covering, a relief. We have a new relationship with God. We are his sons and daughters. We are kept by Jesus, the Prince of Peace.

3. We believe God is our avenger.

The third smooth stone of truth is that God is our avenger. When we are wronged, too many of us want to take matters into our own hands. But God does the avenging for us. Do you believe that?

The reason why the giant of anger must fall in our lives is because it demoralizes us and diminishes the glory of God. How? Because it robs God of his own rightful declaration about who he is. God says, *I am the one who's going to avenge all wrongs.* If we really believe that, then we would say, "Wow, okay, so there legitimately is an injustice here. But God has promised that he's going to avenge what I can't avenge."

Too often the expressions of our anger only throw gasoline on an already burning fire. We lash out at a person. We withhold love or communication or encouragement from a person. We seek to hurt a person back. We think our gasoline is going to make things better, but it only causes things to blow up. When we seek to avenge, we only become more bitter and broken. We can't alleviate what caused the anger in the first place. We can't change people's hearts.

The way we righteously deal with anger is by aligning ourselves with God's justice. He gives us the power to make peace with other people. He is the avenger of all injustice and all wrong in the world. Justice will come. It will either come today on earth or in the future in heaven, but rest assured, justice will come. One day God will right every wrong. And he's going to be fairer about it than you and I could ever be. He's going to be more comprehensive about it. The situation will find true justice, true peace, true reconciliation.

To relinquish avenging to the Lord is not to brush our unresolved conflicts under the rug. There may be a needed step of confrontation, open communication, or restitution. But we must approach any such process from the position of forgiveness. Our release from their wrongful actions will never fully come from man's decision or the outcome of a process. Our freedom comes from anchoring our hope in the fact that our great God defends us and rights all wrongs. Therefore, while we are waiting on God's justice we can operate from forgiveness, not for it.

Paul in Romans 12:14 offers us this counterintuitive instruction: "Bless those who persecute you; bless and do not curse." And in verse 17: "Do not repay anyone evil for evil."

That doesn't sound like how most people today deal with anger, does it? The giant of anger says we need to repay evil with evil. If someone hits us, then we need to hit that person back. Surely that will make us feel better, won't it? Hey, let me know how that goes.

What do you do instead of hitting back?

- *You say you're hurt. Fine. Let Jesus heal that hurt.*
- You say you've been wounded. Fine. Let Jesus deal with your wounds.
- *You say you're aching. Fine. Let Jesus deal with your sorrow and heartbreak.*

God is bigger and more powerful than we can ever imagine. We may be hurt, yes, but Jesus is bigger than our wounds. Jesus is bigger than our sorrows. He is able to "repay you for the years the locusts have eaten" (Joel 2:25). The things that have been destroyed by injustice, Jesus is able to restore fully.

The world tells you to hate and feel wronged and hold a grudge. But Christians are called to walk through the world with the heart of Christ. We offer people a different model. We show people a different picture. Is there a wrong in our past we're still worked up over? Hey, we've known God too long to be bitter about that. We've walked with Jesus too far to still be jacked up about this. The Holy Spirit has filled my heart too much for me to hold that grudge against you. Our God is too big for us to hate others.

Paul says in Romans 12:18, "If it is possible, as far as it depends on you, live at peace with everyone." This is the same guy who had rocks thrown at him. More than once Paul was thrown in prison. Three times he was beaten with rods. Five times he was whipped within an inch of his life. Yet he doesn't call for revenge.

He calls for peace.

4. We forgive.

How does the giant of anger fall? The fourth smooth stone of truth is forgiveness. By Christ's power, we forgive the person we're angry with.

Paul says in Ephesians 4:25–26, "Therefore each of you must

put off falsehood and speak truthfully to your neighbor, for we are all members of one body. 'In your anger do not sin': Do not let the sun go down while you are still angry." In other words, if you take Scripture at its word, then don't go to bed tonight without dealing with any anger still in your heart. Hold out forgiveness to the person who wronged you. When you forgive, you acknowledge the wrong, sure. But you also don't hold it against him or her.

Maybe you wonder how you can do this. The person you're angry with doesn't live close to you. Maybe you're not talking anymore. Maybe that person is dead. Maybe the hurt seems like too much to forgive. You still want to kill this person, not forgive them. I get that. There are some horrible things done in this world. And maybe the pain in your life is so great, you can't even broach the topic of forgiving someone. Yet you've got to let go. You've got to let God shift the tide in your heart. You've got to release the resentment. You've got to release the burden from your back, and the way it's released is through forgiveness.

Forgiveness is when you turn to the Lord in prayer and say, "God, by the grace of Jesus I want you to know I forgive this person. You forgave me. I forgive them. I can't hold against this person more than what you chose not to hold against me." You have the power, because of the cross, to say, "I forgive you." The other person may say, "I don't care." Or "I never did anything wrong." Or "Well, this misunderstanding was all your fault."

That's okay. If they don't want to hear it, then you tell your for-giveness to yourself and God. You release yourself. When you do, the giant stops taunting.

Forgiveness is a process. Sometimes we need to forgive a person more than once. A relationship may not be restored just because you forgive someone. And you might not want that relationship restored. Just because you forgive a person doesn't mean you want to be friends with them anymore. Yes, there are going to be some boundaries in your relationship—and that's okay—but yes, you still want to forgive.

What you want is to be able to lie down tonight in your bed and sleep in peace in the shadow of the cross. You don't want to carry your anger one more day. You want to lie down this very night and say, "Lord, I hold no grudges against anyone, because you hold no grudges against me." In that moment when you for-give, the Devil isn't given a foothold. He can't put another brick in the wall.

5. We remind ourselves we are sons and daughters of God.

The fifth smooth stone of truth is that we've been chosen by a perfect Father. We need to remind ourselves of this daily.

A lot of people's anger can be the result of feeling betrayed and belittled. The person who did the betrayal and belittling was an authority figure, a parent, a teacher, an older relative, or a boss. Yet Jesus' voice speaks above it all. He declares that we are his sons and daughters. He has adopted us. He has chosen us as his own. God is perfect, and we are the children of a good, good Father. In his eyes we are loved and safe, secure and significant because of him. Thanks to Jesus, we have what it takes. Thanks to Jesus, we are loved and adored.

We see David, the giant slayer, reveling in this love of God. David was confident because he had the confidence of Christ in him. David knew the fame of the Lord was at stake, and David didn't rest on his abilities; he rested in the power of God within him. He killed a giant not for the fame of himself but for the fame of God. David wrote these words in Psalm 68:

> *Sing to God, sing in praise of his name,*
> *extol him who rides on the clouds;*
> *rejoice before him—his name is the LORD.*
> *A father to the fatherless, a defender of widows,*
> *is God in his holy dwelling.*
> *God sets the lonely in families,*
> *he leads out the prisoners with singing;*
> *but the rebellious live in a sun-scorched land. (vv. 4–6)*

God is a father to the fatherless and a defender of widows and orphans. That is God in his holy habitation. The giant of anger goes down when we pick up the stone that says we are loved sons and daughters.

Finally Free

One thing's for sure, we live in a broken world, and that gives us plenty of reason to be angry. But being angry and allowing the giant of anger to cut the heart of joy out of our chests are two different things. Living with a smoldering fire is a sorry way to live. Living like a victim is defeating and imprisoning. Sooner or later, we have to get fed up with the giant and take it down.

Aren't you tired of being mad all the time? Weary from holding on to the grudge all these years?

Taking down this giant is really about us letting go of control.

I've always butted heads with the overly simplistic admonition "let go and let God." But it's really quite powerful, and for me, it's the best way forward against the giant of anger. Unresolved anger is deceptive like all sin, causing us to feel for once that we are in control. We think, *I'm not going to forgive. I'm not going to let you get away with it. I'm not going to ever speak to you again. I'm going to make you regret ever doing that to me.* And that feels empowering. Yet half the time the other person is off on a holiday without a care in the world while our stomachs are rotting. We are seething while they are snoozing on a beach somewhere.

For God's sake, we have to get our eyes off of them and back on Jesus. We have to realize that we are held by nail-pierced hands. We have to agree that we are treasured and loved. This affirms that we believe what God did for us is greater than what anyone could do against us. This puts us back together again. This frees us to actually live our lives, to run our race, to bloom and blossom into what God says we can be. To be loved, to let go, to let God extinguish the fire that's threatening to burn our dreams to the ground.

But, there's one more really nasty giant still standing that must come down.

CHAPTER 7

Addiction Must Fall

———

The scene at the restaurant the other night was classic . . . and typical. Sitting at the table next to us was a mom, dad, and three kids. I'm not sure how they ordered and actually ate their food because they were all in their own worlds. Dad was on his phone, apparently answering a few critical e-mails. I could see over Mom's shoulder (don't judge me for being a tad nosey, please), and she was engrossed in Facebook, clicking and commenting with impressive speed as she scrolled through people's lives. One of the kids was playing Candy Crush on his tablet. Another kid was turning his iPad from side to side, playing a racing game. The third kid actually had headphones on at the table with another screen in front of him. He was playing some sort of war game, destroying cities and blowing up people, and every once in a while I could see his eyes light up. Under his breath he'd murmur, "Yes! Goodbye, sucker."

Sadly, this has become our new normal.

We're one of the most overstimulated generations of people in the history of the world. We have nine hundred channels on TV and we're still bored. I remember the day when we had only four channels on TV. Everybody knew what was on, because we all watched the same shows. If we misbehaved as kids, Mom and Dad would send us to our rooms. Strong medicine, right? It was back then. There was no computer in my room. No cell phone. No video game system. No Wi-Fi. No e-mail. No streaming video. No connection to a billion friends on social media. Mom and Dad would send me to my room, and that was considered solitary confinement.

We're an addicted generation. We don't think of ourselves as addicted, but we are. That's a tough blanket to spread, isn't it? Mention the word *addicted* and the tone in a room instantly changes. Our minds connect the word to the "big" addictions only, such as alcoholism, drug abuse, or porn. We think of addicts only as the poor souls who go to rehab. But this generation is addicted to all manner of things. Some stuff little, some stuff big. We always need to have something going on. We've always got to be filling our minds with something to distract and entertain us. A family of five can't spend an hour at the dinner table without the eyes of each person being glued to a different screen. And entertainment is certainly not the only addiction we struggle with today.

Now, I'm certainly not demeaning the process of dealing

We are *able* because God is *able*.

with big addictions. Recently a friend recounted the scene as a mom walked into a circle of desperation she thought was a meeting with a real-estate broker at their home. The meeting was a setup—an intervention. Seated in the circle were her parents, her husband of twenty-four years, her two closest friends, her sister, and three of her children, ages 19, 16, and 14.

The mom was addicted to alcohol and prescription meds. The most gripping moment came when the sixteen-year-old emptied a plastic trash bag filled with empty beer cans and pill bottles she had been scavenging from the waste bin in the garage. "Mom," she asked, "why do you love these more than me?"

In reality, it's likely the mom did not love the meds and the drinks more than her daughter. She was just being squashed by the giant called addiction and it was on the verge of destroying everything and everyone she loved.

The big addictions are real. Our family has been through some huge ones, and if this is your story, I'm right there with you. I'm not taking them lightly. Yet I don't want any of us to sit back and say, "Well, since I'm not struggling with this big addiction, and since I'm not struggling with that big addiction, then I really don't have any addictions in my life."

When it comes to addictions we need to cast a wider net. An addiction is anything we can't live without. We're enslaved to this thing. It's a habit we can't break. It's a person we can't separate from. A pattern we can't change. And it's ultimately harmful. If left unchecked, the addiction devastates our lives and everything around us.

That's the giant of addiction at work. It robs us of our very best. It leads us down a never-ending path to a never-fulfilled promise. And in the end, the giant of addiction stands over us, ridiculing us and dimming the fame and glory of God in our lives.

That's why the giant of addiction must fall.

The Biggest Addiction

———

Addictions are powerful, and addictions are typically illogical—it makes little sense to choose harmful paths, but we do so anyway. The fight against an addiction can go on not just for months but for years. Within this fight it's easy to sink to a place where we say, "Okay, this practice or habit or substance or relationship isn't going to go any further than this. Surely this is the bottom. It can't get any worse." Maybe there's a little glimmer of hope for a season. We battle back against the addiction. Everybody who's cheering for us breathes a sigh of relief. But then we relapse. Or we sink to a new level. If you have been down that roller-coaster road, you know how difficult and frustrating and confusing and scary it can be.

The substance might be different, but the pattern is eerily

similar. For some people, their drug of choice is alcohol. For some it's meth, a completely ruinous drug. For others it's coke. Some think their drug is harmless; it's just a party drug that keeps the fun going all night. The drug of choice could be painkillers, like my friend's sister mentioned above. Oxy gets a lot of news these days. And heroin is leaving carnage everywhere.

Some people are addicted to money. You just can't get enough of it. No matter how much money you have, you need to have more. Other people are addicted to sex. Plenty of people are addicted to porn. We've all seen the statistics. Porn is this huge giant standing up in the middle of the room, shouting its taunt: "You're never going to be free of this." But that's a lie.

Plenty of people are addicted to buying things and getting more stuff. When you can't cope with life, you go to a store. You can't stop yourself, and it doesn't matter if you have money to spend or not. This addiction runs all up and down the socioeconomic chain. Some people are addicted to Nordstrom. Others get their fix at Walmart. There's a reason plenty of stores are open twenty-four hours a day. When people can't deal with life, they just need to get a shopping cart in front of them. This addiction is laughably called "retail therapy." But make no mistake, it's a drug.

Accomplishments can be a drug. You seek a new level of achievement at work. A promotion. An award. A commendation. You were the regional sales manager and now you're moving up the ladder even higher. You were recognized by the panel of judges. You bring home all As and your GPA is 4.0. You take

Advanced Placement classes so your GPA can be 4.1 or 4.2. You always need to come in first. You're always striving to achieve, and you can't handle it if you don't. It all sounds good, but down deep you know that achievement is your drug of choice.

Adrenaline can be a drug for a lot of people. You can't be at rest. You need to be hyped up all the time. You wake up and drink Red Bull for breakfast. You drink a 5-Hour Energy Boost for lunch. A triple shot of espresso for dinner. You don't want your motor to stop and will do anything to avoid the silence.

Some people are addicted to pain. You're caught in a lie. You cut yourself or burn yourself or deliberately put yourself in dangerous or painful situations because that's how you deal with life. A normal day makes you feel numb, so you believe the only way you can cope is by feeling something—anything—and physical pain makes the endorphins flow.

Some people are addicted to people. You need a certain person, and if you don't see this person or hear from this person, then you get out of sorts. You know who you are. You're reading this book right now and glancing at your phone every two minutes and thinking, *Why isn't he texting me? He still hasn't texted me. I don't know why he hasn't texted me. Oh, I sure wish he'd text me!*

> Do you know what the most widespread
> addiction out there is today? It's this:
> the approval of others.

If you just whispered, "Well, I'm not addicted to this," then you actually are. Because why did you want to justify yourself against this claim? Why did you feel compelled to let yourself or anyone around you know that you're not addicted to people's opinions? People who say, "I don't care what you think," are actually saying, "It matters a lot to me what you think—and that's why I'm telling you so strongly that I don't care. Because I *do* care—and I want you to know it!" Hey—we all want to be liked by other people. We all want to be accepted. We all want to know we're not alone in this world.

Social media has figured this out. Social media sticks a knife into the addiction of approval and twists the handle in a big way. It's difficult to mention any specific sites these days because the cool ones change so fast, but as I'm writing this, Instagram and Facebook lead the pack. Soon they will become tomorrow's Myspace, and in their places other social media sites will emerge. But the addiction of approval will still be around.

As mentioned, I like social media overall. I think it can do a lot of great things. It can keep families and friends connected. It helps us celebrate other people's lives. It's a great way to encourage the whole world. We can give glory to God on social media. But it can be harmful too. Have you ever thought anything like this?

Ah, here's a picture of myself I like. It's one of my best photographs ever. I saw my friend's photo of the same thing. She went to Paris and got a good photo of herself at such and such a place, so I got a good photo of myself at such and such a place. I picked a cool photo filter. I just posted my picture to the world. Here I am, people. Celebrate me. Let me know I'm cool. Let me know you love me. How about that?

We post the picture and then we wait.

We wait for the magic "like" button to be hit.

We refresh and wait a minute longer.

Then the first "like" button is hit. We hope for more. *Ah, someone likes my picture. Finally. Anyone else? Come on, people—this is a really cool picture of me. Are all of my friends asleep right now? Did you all instantly go blind?*

That's addiction to approval. If social media is used as a way for people to celebrate others and share life together around the world and talk about Jesus and the gospel, then social media is great. But if social media is where you are getting your approval and if it's your drug, then social media is going to kill you. Tweet that.

We Are All Vulnerable

———

Underneath any addiction (and our foundational need for approval) is a larger question. It's this: What problem is occurring in my life that I need to mask the pain or emptiness with an addiction? See, the drugs or the alcohol or the sex or the porn or the people or the social media or the retail therapy is only a symptom. The cause is something else. The cause lies under the surface.

The root cause of most addictions is pain. The cause is sin. Somebody has rejected us. Somebody has inflicted pain on us— emotional pain, physical pain, relational pain, economic pain. This person has made us feel like we're not good enough. We're convinced we don't have what it takes. A sense of inadequacy has been branded on our lives. Our security and sense of significance have been ripped away. Our world was turned upside down, and nothing makes sense or looks clear or feels right. We are lonely or angry or tired or annoyed or frustrated or fearful or betrayed or lost or disgusted or grieving or knocked off kilter. That's the cause.

The symptom is whatever addiction shows up and promises to make us feel better. See, when we feel chaotic inside, we run to something that promises relief. We feel we need to cope somehow, so we turn to the thing we think will make us feel better. Maybe that addiction actually does deliver relief for a short time. The addiction gives a buzz. A high. A thrill. A rush. But then the addiction lets us down big-time, and we go even lower than before. If you're ravenously hungry and there's pain in your life and food is your addiction, then you might eat a big bagful of Oreos. You might actually feel full afterward. Your head will spin from all the sugar and you'll feel queasy, but you'll still feel full. Your hunger will be alleviated. A bit of the symptom will be eased. But the double-stuffed treat won't truly nourish your body. And the root cause of an addiction to food won't be addressed. If all you eat meal after meal after meal is sugar, then sugar won't truly deliver on its promise. You'll be seriously sick before long. And what's causing you to eat that way in the first place will never get addressed.

We need to look past the symptom and examine the cause. What's the source of the chaos in our lives? Why do we feel so inadequate? Why do we fear being known? Where is the pain coming from? Unless we're willing to look underneath the drug and figure out what's causing the problems in the first place, then the giant of addiction is not going to fall.

It's quite likely that the cause at the bottom of it all is not a thing, but a person. We don't form our feelings in a vacuum. We are shaped by the expectations or rejection of others. We are made to feel inadequate and afraid, and we don't want anyone to know just how weak and isolated we feel.

All this makes us feel vulnerable inside. I'm not talking about the good sort of vulnerability, where vulnerability can be beautiful—like when a person takes an important risk, or steps out in faith, or becomes vulnerable before God. I'm talking about the negative sort of vulnerability. Being vulnerable in this negative sense means we're open to attack. We're interfacing with the chaotic. We're in a car with bald tires on a wet road. We're a normal man facing up to a giant and about to be slaughtered.

Danger is upon us and it feels like danger will win. Our pattern is this: vulnerability makes us feel weak; and weakness makes us try to cover up and cope; and when we try to cover up and cope, we run to an addiction.

Let's put it into practical terms. If someone you know is addicted to porn, then the root cause in the broadest terms is that he or she is feeling "vulnerable." They feel lost. Confused. Open to attack. Under pressure. They are hurt. Bored. Lonely. Feeling rejected. Something along those lines. So they run to this evil as a means of covering up their vulnerability. They run to the addiction hoping it will satisfy. Hoping the pain will go away. But it never does. And he or she gets hurt in the process. Pornography is a destroyer of every good thing. The pornography never satisfies or brings positive results. It's a super-short-term high for an insecure soul. In the end, the addiction brings death to every good thing around us.

Fortunately, there is a solution: Christ. Jesus takes down the giant of our addictions. And we've got to derail this harmful trajectory of turning toward harm whenever we feel pain. Chaos still happens in the world, and we will still fight the feelings of vulnerability. That fight won't stop. We will still want to cover up and cope. But the solution, instead of running to an addiction, is running to Jesus. We can be confident and secure when we're immersed in intimacy with God.

Let's look at David's life for a greater understanding of how this works.

The Mask of Ill-Fitting Armor

When David got ready to engage in battle with Goliath, King Saul told David these straightforward words:

"You are not able." (1 Samuel 17:33)

Saul went on to explain why. He said, "You are not able to go out against this Philistine and fight him; you are only a young man, and he has been a warrior from his youth" (v. 33).

At first glance, that sounds like King Saul was being concerned for David. But I'm not sure it was truly concern. Or complete concern. I think it was Saul's attempt to unmask David. To make David feel vulnerable. King Saul was a big, strong, experienced warrior, a head taller than any other man in the Israelite army. He had a suit of the best armor. He had a full complement of fighting men at his side. King Saul should have been the one to go out and fight Goliath. But he didn't. Whenever Goliath taunted, King Saul stayed in his tent, worrying. I think when a teenage kid, David, came up and declared that he was going to fight the giant, Saul's first reaction was to point out to everybody how difficult it was going to be. How impossible. Saul wanted to save face. He wanted to declare to anyone in hearing distance that fighting a giant was no small matter. The boy was going to fail.

Yet notice what David said to Saul in return. David stayed respectful. He stayed wise. David reminded everyone that he was Saul's servant. He wasn't trying to usurp the king. He actually had good reasons for believing he could go fight the giant. David said,

> "Your servant has been keeping his father's sheep. When a lion or a bear came and carried off a sheep from the flock, I went after it, struck it and rescued the sheep from its mouth. When it turned on me, I seized it by its hair, struck it and killed it. Your servant has killed both the lion and the bear; this uncircumcised Philistine will be like one of them, because he has defied the armies of the living God. The LORD who rescued me from the paw of the lion and the paw of the bear will rescue me from the hand of this Philistine." (vv. 34–37)

Unfortunately, Saul couldn't rest in this proclamation of the goodness of God. Saul had to add to that the thinking of a mere man—himself. So Saul dressed David in the king's own tunic. Saul put a coat of armor on David and a bronze helmet on his head. David fastened Saul's sword over the tunic and tried walking around. But it was awkward. He wasn't used to all that equipment. Saul's armor turned out to be nothing more than a cover-up for what he perceived to be David's inadequacy. Saul wanted David to suit up so David would look stronger and more protected than he really was.

That's us too. We try to put on false armor all the time. We feel powerless in a broken world. We're afraid. We feel open to attack, so we hide, and we hide in addictions. We try to wrap ourselves in things that promise to make us stronger or more protected than our truest selves. Why do people drink before they go to a party? Because for a lot of people alcohol loosens things up and makes them feel more open to social interaction. People say a drink or two makes them feel more comfortable around others. Why? Maybe they are afraid of other people. Or afraid of rejection. They fear they won't receive other people's approval. So they turn to an addiction instead. But David put aside all the trappings that Saul tried to weigh him down with and he turned to the Lord. He went out to fight the giant with just himself, his sling, his rod, and his God. That's the template for our living too.

Covering and Coping

Remember the story of Adam and Eve in the garden of Eden? This story relates to everything we've been talking about. The picture opens up for us in Genesis 2:24–25, a pretty happy union for the first humans. "That is why a man leaves his father and mother and is united to his wife, and they become one flesh. Adam and his wife were both naked." And they were *not* ashamed.

Amen to that. Here were the first two people in the world. Both naked. No shame. That's beautiful. The Bible states clearly that you can be both naked and unashamed, although that doesn't seem to happen much these days. People still get naked with other people, but afterward they both feel ashamed. Yet in God's economy, nakedness and being unashamed go hand in hand. Adam and Eve were created by God. They were joined together in union by God. He knew everything about them. Adam and Eve had no wardrobe problem. No body-image issues. They were in full fellowship with God. But then sin entered the story, and things changed.

In Genesis 3:9, God came down, as he always did, to walk with Adam and Eve in the cool of the evening. He couldn't find them on this particular day, not because he didn't know where they were, but because they didn't know where *they* were. God called out, "Where are you?" Adam answered, "I heard you in the garden, and I was afraid because I was naked; so I hid" (v. 10).

That's exactly what we do when we feel vulnerable in a broken world. We're like, "Man, I don't want people to see me. I'm afraid of what people will think if they see the real me, so I'm going to hide. I'm going to cover up. I'm going to wear somebody else's armor. I don't want to be vulnerable. I don't want people to know I'm not as strong as they think I am. I don't want people to know I'm afraid. I don't want people to know I crave affirmation. I don't want people to know how insecure I am in this moment. So what I'm going to do is cover up my vulnerability because I don't want anybody to see me like this. I better take a drink, because that'll give me some courage. That'll give me peace." As soon as we leave intimacy with God, we leave peace with God and a place with God. Then we get into a hostile environment where we are feeling ashamed and defenseless and are comparing ourselves to other people and feeling like we need to run away or hide. We do crazy things.

God wants us to understand that our vulnerability isn't the worst thing in the world. Whenever we feel vulnerable, God invites us to run to him. In 1 Samuel 17, David had all of Saul's armor on, but David said in the middle of verse 39, "'I cannot go in these,' he said to Saul, 'because I am not used to them.'" David took off Saul's armor. He pulled off the false cover. He walked out to battle as his real self. He was able to defeat the giant because he was confident in his intimacy with God. David still might have felt vulnerable, but he wasn't alone. His God was way bigger than the giant. David called out to Goliath in verses 45–46: "You come against me with sword and spear and javelin, but I come against you in the name of the LORD Almighty, the God of the armies of Israel, whom you have defied. This day the LORD will deliver you into my hands."

One of the beautiful things about this word—*vulnerable*—is that right within the middle of the word we see this promise . . .

Vulner**ABLE**

With God, we are able. We are able because God is able. Thanks to our vulnerability, we are weak. But thanks to God, we are strong.

More Grace Addicts, Please

The word *vulnerable* offers us another big opportunity. When we look at the first letter of the word, we can remember which way to turn. Here's what I mean: We've used the word in a negative sense in this chapter; being vulnerable means we're open to attack. Yet look at the letter *V*, the letter at the start of the word. Imagine the *V* is made up of two arrows joined at the bottom. These arrows point upward in two different directions. One arrow goes one way. One arrow goes another.

Route one is our decision to lean into the negative side of vulnerability and feel unable and inadequate. Going this direction takes us to the end of our rope. We want to hide and cover up and get some kind of drug to help us cope.

Route two is our decision to lean into the person of Jesus. Whenever we feel vulnerable, we acknowledge our weaknesses and run to Jesus. We don't try to cover up and cope. We don't seek something harmful in an attempt to ease our lack of peace or to give us a buzz. We just run to Jesus as fast as we can. In him, we find the freedom to be "naked and unashamed" with our loving Creator. We come to him just as we are. No hiding. No masking. No pretending we're anything other than our real selves. Jesus knows. He loves us. He calls us his beloved sons and daughters. In Jesus, we are forgiven. In Jesus, we are redeemed. In Jesus, we are loved. In Jesus, we are safe.

If there's anything good that can come from our harmful addictions, it's that they remind us we were created to be dependent creatures. Sin puffs us up and makes us think we are independent—that we control our own destinies. But we were created by and for God. There is a God-sized hole in our souls that can only be filled with an intimate and real relationship with Jesus.

Addiction is not bad, if we reroute our cravings toward something (Someone) good.

What does this actually look like, this running to Jesus when we feel vulnerable? It's when we go to Jesus in prayer and say, "I admit it, Lord. I'm weak. I'm vulnerable. This is what's true of me. Jesus, I'm having a hard time right now. Jesus, I feel very open to attack right now. Jesus, I am weak but you are strong. Jesus, by your grace I can overcome." And Jesus blesses this honesty. He blesses this intimacy with him. We find joy because Jesus embraces us as we are. Jesus doesn't push us away. He accepts us in his love, and he infuses us with his life. We exchange our weakness for his strength. When we are vulnerable, Jesus is *ABLE*.

This is what it looks like to be addicted to the grace of God. I freely exchange any of my addictions for my addiction to Jesus.

Sure, I long for people's approval. I'm addicted to worry. Addicted to fear. Yet Christ lives in me, and because of him I truly live. Because of Jesus, my giants have fallen. If I try to cover up my weaknesses or go to a drug and try to cope, then that only harms me. It destroys the life God wants for me. But when I run to Jesus, I experience his infusing life and power. I exchange my weakness for his strength. I freely admit I'm a grace addict—someone attached to the person and work of Jesus. I love to be with Jesus. I love to talk about Jesus. I lean on Jesus. I trust in Jesus. I love to be filled up with the love of Jesus. I hope in Jesus. I live for Jesus. Because of Jesus I truly live. I can't get enough of Jesus.

If you ask me, the church needs a whole lot more grace addicts because grace has a name, and the name is Jesus. There are people in any church who will drive to the worst part of the city and risk their well-being to get a harmful fix. We see these stories in the news. These beautiful, smart, amazing kids in our city end up dead on the side of the road from a heroin overdose. Housewives are living double lives—alive at church, but dead in their addictions to painkillers. Businessmen are living lives of shame—present at a men's breakfast at their church, but harboring infidelity on the side. It doesn't matter who you are or where you come from, people will do the craziest things to get their drugs. The answer to all this is to become addicted to Jesus.

Being a grace addict is a good thing, not a bad thing. As soon as somebody gets too excited about Jesus, we start calling them a

Jesus freak, and we act like this is a bad thing. But what we need in the church today are lots and lots more Jesus freaks. Those who say, "Jesus, you are my only hope, and I'm clinging to you my whole life long."

Jesus Died Alone, but We Fight in Packs

Probably the greatest lie of all when we're facing our addictions is that we can wage the battle on our own. Because our sin, shame, inadequacy, and fear have us in a cover-up, we want to work ourselves free in the privacy of our own lives. We're afraid of being known, of being honest, of being vulnerable. But the *ABLE* comes with being honest with God and with those around us.

When Jesus called Lazarus out of the grave, he still wasn't completely free. He was miraculously alive, yet he was still bound by the strips of burial linen that had been layered around his body in death. Lazarus stumbled out of the tomb at the command of Jesus, but then Jesus gave instructions to the people:

"Unwrap him and let him go!" (John 11:44 NLT)

How many times have you felt something powerful in your heart and promised God everything would change? In a moment of surrender you swore you'd never return to your drug again. You were convinced you'd walk differently from that point on. But the layers of addictive behavior still encased you in a cocoon of defeat, and much sooner than you thought, your promises were swirling down the drain.

"What happened?" you ask. "I thought this giant was *dead*!"

Because of Christ, the giant is done. And more, you're intentions were strong. It wasn't your desire that failed you. It wasn't your plan that let you down. Your plan was to keep things on the down low. Not to tell anyone. Deal with it yourself. Keep things in the dark.

But freedom happens in the light. Jesus is the Light of the World, and he works most powerfully in us when we bring our brokenness and hurt, or sin and our drugs, into the light of his grace. If we don't, we can fool those around us, but they will never truly know us. This cycle of never being known drives us deeper into the vortex of the cover-up and makes us anemic. We don't want to take the "hit" of coming clean, or maybe we just can't quite admit we are addicted in the first place. But in the end we are isolated by our inability to open up to the love of God and the help of others.

You are free in Christ the instant you place your trust in him. But it may be that you need to call on those standing close by to help unravel the layers. Outside help could look like rehab. It might take the shape of counseling. It will for sure involve accountability in the context of friendship, tough love mixed with grace that will not let you go down to the empty well again.

Until you are willing to find a pack and surround yourself with an ecosystem of support, the giant will loom large and you'll never be known, or free. Do whatever is necessary to weave your life into a system of openness, honesty, and accountability. Until you are okay with being seen as needy or weak, you will never walk in true strength.

When I Am Weak, Then I Am Strong

Paul wrote powerful words in 2 Corinthians 12:7–10. He was able to deliver these powerful words because he first gave a confession about his specific weakness.

> To keep me from becoming conceited, I was given a thorn in my flesh, a messenger of Satan, to torment me. Three times I pleaded with the Lord to take it away from me. But he said to me, "My grace is sufficient for you, for my power is made perfect in weakness." Therefore I will boast all the more gladly about my weaknesses, so that Christ's power may rest on me. That is why, for Christ's sake, I delight in weaknesses, in insults, in hardships, in persecutions, in difficulties. For when I am weak, then I am strong.

Here's the picture. Paul was able to do some amazing things for Christ. But to keep him from becoming conceited, God allowed a thorn in his flesh. We don't know exactly what this thorn was, but it was something adversarial. Did Paul have an illness? Was it his singleness? Was it blindness? Was it somebody dogging him the whole time? Theologians debate exactly what it was. But what we know for sure is God allowed it to be there.

You're like, "Okay. You just lost me. Why would God put a thorn in anybody's flesh? Isn't God's plan to bless me and not to curse me, to give me a future and a hope?" Yes, it is. When God allowed the thorn in Paul's flesh, God wasn't trying to hurt Paul. God wanted to make Paul stronger. God was trying to help Paul understand that the power supply available to him was actually much greater than he thought. Sure, Paul didn't want the thorn there. Three times Paul prayed for God to remove it. But Jesus said to Paul, "My grace is sufficient for you, for my power is made perfect in weakness."

That's an example of how weakness can be our friend. Vulnerability can actually be an asset as we walk with God into the Valley of Elah (whatever our specific valley is). That's why Paul said, "I will boast all the more gladly about my weaknesses." That's the path of the *V* that Paul chose. He wasn't trying to hide his weaknesses from everyone. He wasn't looking for a drug to numb himself. Instead, he boasted about his weaknesses so Christ's power would rest on him. Everyone who has ever done something great for God had some sort of weakness. All the great people of the faith walk with a limp, and the answers for why are throughout Scripture.

- Jacob wrestled with God and he limped the rest of his life. Yet Jacob became the father of the twelve tribes of Israel.
- Peter balked under pressure. He denied Christ big-time. Yet Jesus raised Peter up and made him an anchor of his church.
- John was thrown into exile on the island of Patmos. He lived there his entire life doing slave labor in a rock quarry. Yet Jesus raised John up. He was given glimpses of heaven and wrote the book of Revelation.
- Paul was blinded by his initial encounter with Jesus on the Damascus Road. Yet Jesus raised Paul up, and he ended up writing a lot of the New Testament.
- The brow of Jesus was pierced with a thorny crown. Jesus was whipped and scourged and crucified on a cross between two thieves. Yet God the Father raised him up from death to life. The drops of blood on Jesus' brow released the drops of blood that liberate you and me.

God would never abuse anyone, but he does allow things in our lives that stick in our sides. But it's only so we can be put in a position where we experience more of the power of God. One of the most often misquoted lines of 2 Corinthians 12:10 is the very last line. Paul said, "For when I am weak, then I am strong."

Maybe you thought you read that wrong. You've always heard it this way: "For when I am weak, then *God* is strong." That's true. God is strong. But Paul says, "I."

I am strong. I am strong because Christ's power lives in me.

Do you want to be strong? Do you want to be a stronger student, a stronger husband, a stronger wife, a stronger parent, a stronger employee, a stronger leader? Do you want to be a stronger church builder? Then celebrate your weakness by admitting your vulnerability. Let Jesus embrace you as you are. Let him accept you in his love. Let Jesus infuse his strength into your life. Allow Jesus to give you the power to exchange your weakness for his strength. Then you'll be walking on supernatural waters. Jesus will invite you then to do things you could not do on your own. The power will come from God. Yet you will have the power.

And you're going to need a battle plan.

CHAPTER 8

A Table in the Presence

—

The plotline twist of this book is that Jesus is David in the story of David and Goliath.

It's ironic—because the giant called Goliath was taken down by a shepherd boy named David. Ironic because Jesus describes himself as our Shepherd many times throughout Scripture. And he promises to lead, guide, and protect us—not in the absence of our foes, but in the *presence of our enemies*. That's the irony—the outcome is the opposite of what's expected. While we are praying something like, "God, get me out of the Valley of Elah," God is keeping us there, yet he is sending a Shepherd to deliver us right smack in the middle of the fight.

That Shepherd, and what he promises us in this moment, is best described in David's own words from Psalm 23.

The LORD is my shepherd, I lack nothing.

He makes me lie down in green pastures,

he leads me beside quiet waters,

he refreshes my soul.

He guides me along the right paths

for his name's sake.

Even though I walk

through the darkest valley,

I will fear no evil,

for you are with me;

your rod and your staff,

they comfort me.

You prepare a table before me

in the presence of my enemies.

You anoint my head with oil;

my cup overflows.

Surely your goodness and love will follow me

all the days of my life,

and I will dwell in the house of the LORD

forever.

There is so much hope for us in this psalm, and notice how the Shepherd gives us what we need right in the midst of the fight. Verse 5 tells us that God wants to spread a feast of provision before us in the very presence of our enemies. While the pressure and the darkness close in, while our giants stand

and taunt us, Jesus wants to show us that he can provide everything we need to survive and successfully navigate the journey through the darkest valley.

Most of us, if we had some advanced input in Psalm 23, would prefer verse 5 read, "He prepares a table before me in *his* presence." We want out of the furnace as quickly as possible. But it's interesting that God doesn't promise that he will hit the Eject button every time we are surrounded by hardship, trial, and challenge. He promises something even more powerful and stunning. Right in the midst of the fray, in full view of the things that are threatening us, our Shepherd spreads a table of provision for us. It's a table for two. One seat for you and one seat is for the God who is for you.

That's good news if you know you're in a fight. And if you sense your giant has the upper hand.

Satan is described in 1 Peter 5 as an enemy who "prowls around like a roaring lion looking for someone to devour" (v. 8). Note, he's not actually a lion; he just roars like one to intimidate you. The Devil wants you to think he has control. He wants to make you feel helpless and hopeless. He wants you to give in to the temptation to believe that things will never change. But as we have seen, he is the one who is defeated. His days are numbered. His head is severed.

Jesus is, in fact, the Lion of Judah. His roar rules the nations. His voice shatters the Enemy. But for a short while, the spiritual fight rages on planet Earth, and Satan prowls and roars and looks for a crack or a crevice through which he can insert himself into our minds, and thus our situations. If you don't stop him, then he'll be sitting at your table.

That reminds me of a beautiful night turned extremely awkward a few years ago as Shelley and I were having a nice dinner at a restaurant in London. Her birthday had just passed, and we were having a celebration at a place we love in the West End. After a brief wait we were seated at a "four top," a table that could accommodate four people. Thus, it was the two of us and two empty chairs.

About twenty minutes into our meal, a young guy leaving the restaurant walked by our table, did a double take, and came back to say hi. He recognized us from an event I'd spoken at a few months earlier in Chicago. We were genuinely happy to meet him and hear how our lives had intersected in God's great kingdom plan. But we were surprised and unprepared for what happened next.

About five minutes after our brief chat, he came back into the restaurant to our table, pulled out one of the empty chairs across from us, and sat down. Before I could blink he was comfortably seated, both arms on the table as he leaned in with a huge grin. He boldly announced that he thought it was amazing that God had connected us and he hoped it was okay if he joined us for the night.

What?

I totally understood his heart (he saw this as an obvious sign from God that we were supposed to discuss something he had been wanting to talk with me about for months), but now I was in a jam. This was supposed to be a special night for just Shelley and me. But now there were three of us at our celebration dinner, though the reservation was *clearly* for two.

I mentioned that it was her birthday and we were celebrating, hoping that would do the trick.

Nope.

He glanced at Shelley and said, "That's cool. Happy birthday!"

Then he shifted his gaze back my way and began what I perceived was going to be a lengthy conversation.

I checked my spirit to see if God wanted us to have this conversation right then. Then I gently had to ask our new friend to allow us to continue our dinner alone. Awkward.

Please understand that the point of this story is not about the well-meaning young man in London. He was nice as could be and we were grateful to meet him (although we were not going to have a special dinner together). The point is about how fast the Enemy can pull up a chair at the table that Jesus has prepared for you. With a big smile and overt confidence, the Enemy strolls into the moment, and before you know it you're having a conversation with a killer. He's sitting at your table. And if he's at your table, then the first thing he's probably telling you is that God's not good and that you can't trust him. As we've seen earlier in this book, that's what Satan said on day one in the garden. He undermined the character of God and made Eve think there was something better that she was missing, something God was withholding from her.

In the midst of your fight, the Enemy will most likely add this dagger—*If God is so good, then why has all this hardship and pain come into your life?*

That question gains traction because we all deal with real pain. Pain is universal. Every person feels pain. Pain is pain is pain. And pain is always valid to the person feeling the pain. Our hearts are genuinely broken, and in our pain we often don't respond all too well to logic and we become subject to the lies of the Enemy sitting in our midst.

We read in Scripture that God is good. That's logical, and we agree with that. We know in our hearts that God has everything under control. Yes, we agree with that. We know that "in all things God works for the good of those who love him, who have been called according to his purpose" (Romans 8:28). No problem there. We believe that God redeems all things, and one day our pain will be alleviated. Sure. One day all injustice will turn to justice. One day all sorrow will be replaced by rejoicing. All that's good and well. Yet the problem is even though we know all those things, we can't move forward. We just can't accept that God is on our side, walking through the valley with us. We know the truth, but logic alone won't convince us that the truth will set us free. Or if we do respond to logic, then we make the mistake of listening with our ears only, and not listening with our hearts.

What do we do?

It All Comes Together

In this chapter, I want to bring everything together for us. I want to keep using biblical logic, because everything good is found in biblical logic. And I want to see if I can help nudge some of us over the line to the place where the truth burrows into all areas of our being: our minds and hearts and souls and lives. Some sort of giant is taunting us. Some sort of pain is in our lives. Some sort of chaos is robbing God's glory in our lives and preventing us from living the abundant life God invites us to live. So how do we actually get from point A to point B? How do we turn the tables and ensure that our giants will actually fall?

For one, we decide here and now that we are not going to give the Devil a seat at our table. Our Shepherd prepares a table before us in the presence of our enemies, and we get to decide who sits at the table or not. By the power of the Holy Spirit, we get to decide who joins that special meal and who gets to be a part of that fellowship.

A few years ago I was going through a stressful season relationally. I texted a close friend to vent my frustration about something that had happened. Something that had been said about me. After a paragraph of my *woe is me* text, I got a one-line response:

Don't give the Enemy a seat at your table.

Wow. That pretty much ended the exchange. I became convicted and confident all at once. Convicted that the text I had just typed was a retelling of the crud the Enemy had been telling me. And confident that in Christ I had the ability to excuse the Enemy from my table. I was the only one responsible for entertaining his thoughts. And I had the power to ignore them.

That's what this chapter is about. I want us to stop the negative news. Stop the Devil's talking. Stop the pain of the immediacy, and take a seat at God's great table. We'll sit down and be still, and just let the breath of our heavenly Father breathe with us. He's the one who invites us to come to him whenever we are weary and heavy-laden. He's the one who gives us rest (Matthew 11:28). When we look at the life of Jesus, we see sometimes he directly taught people, but he also went beyond direct teaching and really helped his hearers put flesh around those ideas. Today he does the same thing. He speaks to the totality of our minds and hearts and souls and lives.

When he does, my encouragement to you is this:

Don't give the Enemy a seat at your table.

So how do you know if the Enemy is sitting at your table? Most of his lies fall in four main groupings.

1. If the Enemy is at your table, then you think you're not going to make it.

Remember, according to Psalm 23, the table is in the presence of your enemies, not the absence of your foes. So the Devil can quickly spin your head around and remind you that you're surrounded on every side. When he does, he says to you: *You're not going to make it. It's not going to end well for you. You're finished. You'll never make it back to where you once were. You'll never win this fight. You'll never be free. Just quit believing all this "my giant is dead" mumbo jumbo and give up. You're done.*

But remember the psalm says that you have a Lord who is your Shepherd who has set a table for two. Let the Shepherd speak to you. Lock onto his words and let them sink in. Notice David wrote "when I walk *through* the valley." He knew his future was not stuck in the middle of the valley, but that his Shepherd would lead him through to the other side. There would be green pasture, quiet water, and rest for his soul on the other side. And there was a table of provision with all he needed in the midst of the fray.

You are not going to die in this barren, defeated place. And if you think you are, then I encourage you—don't give the Devil a seat at your table.

2. If the Enemy is at your table, then you think there's something better at another table.

He tempts you with thoughts like these:

Look over there.

Hey, the party's at that other table. It's way more fun over there.

You got a raw deal at your table.

That's going to make your pain go away.

Being at a different table is definitely going to make you feel better.

God left you in the dark valley. Ditch him and just go do whatever you want!

Satan is after God's glory. He refuses to honor the Almighty and targets anyone he can deceive in an effort to strike at the very heart of God. He's not just out to get you; he's out to tarnish God's glory because we were created in the image of God with extraordinary purpose and promise. You are God's prized possession. If Satan can gash your heart, he can break the heart of God.

There's nothing on your horizon better than Jesus. Any sales job that seeks to convince you otherwise is an empty lie. Jesus is committed to the very best for you and will never withhold from you what is good.

If you're tempted to bail on your Shepherd (or you're currently at another table), then I encourage you—don't give the Devil a seat at your table.

3. If the Enemy is at your table, then you feel like you're not good enough for God.

The Enemy tempts you with thoughts like these:

You don't matter.

You've never mattered to anyone.

God doesn't care about you.

You don't deserve a table with God.

God doesn't love you anymore. In fact, he never loved you in the first place.

You are too far away from God. God's finished with you. There is no way back.

Yet the context of Psalm 23 helps us see that at the time of its writing, the word *table* meant "feast." Only important, prominent people were able to afford throwing a feast. And important people would only invite other important people to their table. So when God prepares a table for you, that means he puts out the deluxe spread (everything you need to survive spiritually, mentally, and emotionally) and invites you to dine with him. He invites you because he cares for you. He invites you because he has already given everything for you.

Jesus gives us a similar promise in John 10:11: "I am the good shepherd. The good shepherd lays down his life for the sheep." Feelings will tell you that you don't matter . . . no one cares about you. Yet the cross of Jesus disrupts that faulty storyline with the greatest display of worth you will ever receive. You are not invisible. You are seen and treasured by the God of the universe.

If you have come to think differently, may I encourage you—don't give the Devil a seat at your table.

4. If the Enemy is at your table, then you think everyone is out to get you.

While there may legitimately be someone in your family or work or school who is saying bad things about you that aren't true and undermining you in some way, paranoia typically comes from the pit of hell.

Have you had the Enemy tell you things such as these?

No one likes you.

Everyone is against you.

Everybody is talking smack behind your back.

They are all scheming to take you out.

You better watch your back.

Here's a question for you: If our Good Shepherd leads us, and if his goodness and love follow us all the days of our lives, then why would we as his sheep ever feel the need to watch our backs? That kind of thinking doesn't come from the Shepherd, but from the Enemy camped at our table. The paranoia bred by the Enemy quickly causes us to assume a defensive posture, believing that everyone is out to get us. Soon this becomes a self-fulfilling prophecy, as we mistrust and attack everyone around us.

I better get them before they get me, we think. And with hands clenched, and a suspecting lens that turns every look into a glare and every unintended lack of notice into a hateful snub, we begin to take on the world. Soon we are caught in a downward spiral of mudslinging that's completely contrary to the gospel of grace that empowers us to love "real" enemies and turn the other cheek.

Why would we turn the other cheek?

Because we are sitting at the table with the Creator of the world. Even if "everyone" is against us (and they are usually not),

Don't give the enemy a *seat* at your table.

Christ's table provides all we need to make it through this season of life, thriving right in their line of sight.

God wants us to focus less on who it is that's surrounding us and focus more on the fact that he is sitting with us. His presence at our table is greater than the presence of any enemy that surrounds us.

God's got your back.

If you feel like you are in a fight against people you know, may I encourage you—don't give the Devil a seat at your table.

Pray and Proceed

Yes, our giants can fall. In fact, our giants *must* fall—which is the whole point of this book. It's a mandate. God's plan for our lives far exceeds the circumstances of our days. Our giants have already fallen, because Jesus has made them fall. That's why they must also fall today. That's a tricky concept, isn't it? It's tricky because we need to contend with this now-and-not-yet reality. Our snakes are dead, but they keep on wriggling. Satan has been defeated at the cross, but the Devil is still prowling.

Our giants keep taunting us, so we need to hold God at his word: that he is already victorious. We need to believe that our pain can be overcome. We need to remind ourselves that those giants don't need to be giants any longer.

This is true for us no matter our stage of spiritual growth. It's imperative that we live in the finished work that Jesus has done for us. Some of you haven't walked with Jesus for very long and that's fine—Jesus invites you forward. Some of you are still figuring out who Jesus is, and you're brand new to all of this; that's fine too. Jesus says, "I want you to be free!" Others of you are mature believers. You're walking with the Lord. You're full of sound teaching. You've been to a lot of church gatherings in your life. You've been to conferences and retreats, you've read a lot of books, and you've seen a lot of video series. You want to move forward in your relationship with Jesus too. Good. No matter what stage any of us are in, it's vital that we don't allow the Enemy to get a foothold in our lives. Why?

Because some sort of sin or addiction might look small on the front end of things. But five or ten or fifteen years later, there's a huge giant in our lives we need to contend with. We've made the mistake along the way of accommodating our giants. We've allowed the giant's false words to speak to us and demoralize us. We've said, "God can do everything else in the world, but I don't know if he can take this giant down." The title of this book is specifically titled *Goliath Must Fall*, with the emphasis on the *must*. It's a decree. God wants us to live free from the demoralizing voice of that giant, and because God wants to get glory in our lives by showing the world that he is greater than everything we face in our lives, then that giant's got to go down.

Your invitation is to pray and proceed and listen to the voice of Jesus. Listen for the voice of your Shepherd. I don't know what your specific giant is, so the applications are always open-ended, dependent upon your specific situation and upon the power of the Holy Spirit in your life. But, rest assured, your giant's got to go. No more accommodating. No more excuse giving. The time is now.

Let's see what might it look like for the Shepherd to lead you.

1. Make sure you are spiritually alive.

We need to make sure we really have Jesus in our lives. It's as simple as that. John lays it out for us: "Whoever has the Son has life; whoever does not have the Son of God does not have life" (1 John 5:12). Do you know you have Jesus in your life? To ask it another way, is Jesus *your* Shepherd? Are you one of his sheep? He says, "My sheep listen to my voice . . . and they follow me" (John 10:27). If not, why not decide to follow Jesus right here, right now, today?

In following Jesus, we realize we fall short of the glory of God. God is perfect, and he can't have anything to do with sin, so we are initially separated from God. Spiritual death overtakes us. But the good news is that Jesus Christ came to earth. He was born as a baby in Bethlehem. He lived on earth for thirty-three years. He was crucified. He definitely died. He was buried in a borrowed tomb. And then Jesus was definitely raised to life again, all so we can have life. God loves the world so much that he gave his only Son to us. Whoever believes in Jesus will not perish but have abundant and eternal life (John 3:16).

"What must I do to be saved?" the Philippian jailer asked Paul and Silas (Acts 16:30). It's a great question, one people are still asking today. The simple answer follows in Scripture: "Believe in the Lord Jesus, and you will be saved," Paul said to him (v. 31). It's that straightforward. Yet this kind of belief is more than simply mentally ascribing to something as true. It's putting all your trust in Jesus to be all he says he can be in your life.

Do we want giants to fall in our lives? Putting our trust in him as Savior and Lord is the first step in having a relationship with an alive, living, communicating, resurrected Jesus who loves us and cares for us and is intimately involved in our lives. That's how we start to depend on Jesus. That's how the giants go down. We make sure we're spiritually alive. We return to the gospel and rally around the cross. We recognize that God is pursuing us with relentless passion. He's fully expressing to us his unfathomable love through the mercy and grace and forgiveness of the cross of his Son, Jesus Christ. Our call is to respond to this and follow the person of Jesus.

Have you done that? If not, do it right now. Pray this prayer with me.

> "Lord Jesus, God Almighty, please save me from my sins.
> I know I fall short of your glory.
> But I don't want there to be any distance between you and me anymore.

I believe that you gave your life on the cross to pay for my sins.

I believe that you rose in victory from the grave.

Please forgive me for all my sin.

Wash all the guilt and shame away.

Jesus, make me alive in you.

I receive you as my Savior and Lord,

And I want to follow you all the days of my life.

Thank you for finding me and saving me.

I believe it. I receive it.

Amen."

2. Let the Shepherd lead you day by day.

To allow God to lead our lives feels counterintuitive to our natural state. We all think we're pretty good at calling the shots and setting the course for our lives. We don't love it when others try to supervise and suggest ways we might live happier, healthier, and more peaceful lives.

Yet the imagery of Psalm 23 is not meant to be flattering to you and me. Being referred to as a sheep is not a compliment. Sheep, by nature, are not the smartest of creatures and don't fare well without oversight and direction.

Notice the first thing the Shepherd does in this psalm—he makes us lie down in green pastures. Typically, we don't like to be made to do anything. Yet our good God will prompt us to do a lot of things. He's not looking for control or power in our lives. He's seeking to lead us to what truly satisfies.

Freedom from our giants begins with humility before God. Daily we come to him and admit we need his help. We breathe out our inability and breathe in his all-sufficiency. We connect the pathways of our lives to his voice and ask him to steer us through the valley to the other side.

Some years ago my friend Marc and I set out to scale the Matterhorn. Though we had no experience in mountaineering, nor knowledge that the mountain of our choosing was one of the deadliest climbs out there, we arrived in the little village of Zermatt, Switzerland, brimming with confidence. Privately, I knew I had *not* crushed our training regimen, but somehow things always seemed to work out for me, so I assumed that would be the case this time. That is until I came face-to-face with the mountain. *How,* I thought, *are we possibly going to get up that thing?*

After a week of altitude acclimatization and further training, we were cleared by the Swiss mountaineering guides to proceed. I was still unsettled, except that our training guide kept saying, "Don't worry. It's a 'walk up.' We'll go super slow, and all you need to do is put one foot in front of the other."

I took comfort in those words and kept repeating them to myself.

Jesus defeated our giants with one fatal blow on the cross. He destroyed their power as he blasted out of the grip of death. The way we walk in that freedom is by believing each day that he will lead us as we put one foot in front of the other. Most times in our lives the power is not in a massive leap but in the succession of a thousand tiny steps.

3. Trust him and lean in his direction.

We've already talked about depending on Jesus to slay the giants for us. Our responsibility is to lean into him. It's a both/and situation. Jesus has already accomplished what he is going to do. We're still in process, so Jesus is processing his victory through us. Yes, Jesus does the real work, and we trust that he does that. And yes, we agree with him. We align our wills with him. That means we follow him. We pray that the giants will fall in Jesus' name and act as though they already have.

We must always combine "leaning" with "trusting." Jesus is still working out his finished work in the process of our work. That's the beauty of a big theological word called *sanctification*. It's God working through us what he has already accomplished. It's God perfecting *in* us what he's already perfected *for* us. So any avenue to change requires our will working in combination with the power of the Holy Spirit. A surfer must paddle in the direction of the wave. The wave does the actual work of taking the surfer back to shore, but the surfer must give himself to the power of the wave and paddle in its direction.

As you paddle along with the wave of God's Spirit, there might be any number of specific actions you need to take. You might need the help of a professional counselor. Maybe the problem will be best worked out within a trusted group of friends, such as in a community group at your church. Maybe confession and even restitution will play a big role in your giants falling. Maybe it's you and Jesus and a journal, working this out together. Maybe a physical issue is compounding the problem, and there's some medication you need to take for a season. There's nothing wrong with using the full arsenal of tools at your disposal.

I don't want to offer you a specific formula for success, because I don't know the specifics of your situation. And I acknowledge that things can and do get worked out in individual lives in different ways as we go forward with Christ. Because that's who it all comes back to—Jesus. He always does the real sanctifying work in our lives. We go his direction. We trust in Jesus, and we lean his direction.

4. Say yes to the Holy Spirit as a way of life.

It's been said we don't ever lose a bad habit; we simply replace it with a better one. That's how we break the cycle of the bad thoughts and actions in our lives. We don't just wish our giants away; we say yes to our Shepherd as he speaks to us and leads us step by step.

Jesus has given us the gift of the Holy Spirit to guide us on the journey. The Spirit is the third person of the trinity—God the Father, Son, and Holy Spirit. He is not an "it"; he is God. And he is Christ's gift to us, the ever-present indwelling person of the life and power of Christ.

We are encouraged toward this end: "Walk by the Spirit, and you will not gratify the desires of the flesh" (Galatians 5:16). Those same old desires will always be there, giants demanding that we cower and fall. Yet the way we say no to their voices is by saying yes to his. The Spirit speaks and nudges our hearts in the direction of life, truth, and freedom. We can say no so many times that we grow calloused to his leading, or we can choose to say yes time and time again and grow more sensitive to his prompting.

Marc and I spent the night high on the Matterhorn after a grueling hike to the base camp the day before. We walked out the door of the Hörnli Hut before dawn the next day and were immediately tethered to our respective guides with 120 feet of rope. Harness to harness, we were connected as we stepped into the cold, dark morning for the 4,300-foot ascent to the summit. In my head I repeated what my training guide had told me. *It's a "walk up." We'll go super slow, and all you need to do is put one foot in front of the other.* But about five minutes in, that mantra vaporized as we encountered a fifty-foot wall of rock with a fixed rope hanging down. The wall went straight up like the side of a building. My guide, Richard (different from the one I had trained with), disappeared into the darkness. Before I lost sight of him he said with an even tone, "I'll get up and get secure. When you feel me tug on the rope, climb behind me."

What? When you get where? Climb on what?

A minute or two later a little jolt hit my harness. So I grabbed the rope and started hoisting myself upward. Our starting point that morning at the Hörnli Hut was at 10,700 feet, so every breath was a piece of work. I pulled with all my might.

As it turned out, this sequence repeated itself in various forms for the next four hours. We'd get to a hard spot in the climb. Richard would vanish. I'd feel the sometimes not-so-gentle tug on my harness. I'd get moving. Soon we'd reconnect and repeat.

You may not be able to see the top of the mountain from where you are, but that's okay. You may not even be able to conceive of making it ten steps up your mountain, much less four thousand vertical feet. But your Shepherd will do the leading. He's ahead of you right now. Secure and able to support you if you should slip, he gives you the go-ahead. Take a step. You might be shocked that you can take that step, given that the Enemy keeps telling you that you can't. You are inseparably linked to Jesus and constantly led by his Spirit.

When the tug from the Spirit comes, say yes. A lot. You'll be amazed at what you can scale. What you can overcome.

5. Make sure you don't take no for an answer.

Complacency is an attitude of the heart. In all honesty, some of us *like* our giants. They've been in our lives for so long they've become part of the landscape. We know in our minds that the giants need to go, but there's security in having those giants there. They're harmful, but they're familiar, and we tend to like what's familiar. But familiarity can be the voice of the Accuser in our lives. Our giants constantly tell us no. *No, I won't fall. No, it can't be done. No, you can't win the victory.*

Don't take no for an answer.

The cross is a safe place, but it's not always a comfortable place. We are in a fight. And when we desire for our giants to fall, when we want the glory and fame of Jesus to be known above all, we want our lives to count for his glory. We drive a stake through the heart of self. We make a determined choice to die to our harmful desires. We make a conscious choice to follow Jesus wholeheartedly.

This has to become personal for each of us. You have to think: *I've got to get rid of my giants. I can't settle into complacency. I've got to see that this giant is a problem. This thing isn't helpful—not ultimately. This thing is trouble. This thing slows me down. This thing kills my relationships. This thing hardens my heart. This thing will destroy me. There's a desperation and an urgency I need to tap into here. I've got to get rid of this thing because I don't want it to kill me. I don't want it to sap the life out of me. I don't want it to destroy every good thing in my life, my relationships, my future, my career, my family. I've got to get rid of this thing—and I've got to get rid of it now!*

Yes, the battle is won, but we are still in a fight. Yes, we're resting in the work of God, but we must go forward and overcome our complacency. And it's not just for our sake either. I mean, come on, we're living on a planet with billions of people who've never heard of Jesus. This world is rattling at the hinges right now. Any day this whole thing could just go up in smoke. But we have the answer: Jesus Christ. There's work to be done. There isn't time to be complacent. We know hope. We have the truth. We have the life. We have the way. We have Jesus.

I don't know how much is waiting on you today, but I do know it's not all about you. There are other people waiting on you to take that step of faith today. I don't know who they are or what they look like or what God's been putting on your heart. But I do know that Jesus wants you to live in the mission he's designed for you. When we follow Christ, his pathway forward begins with us trusting in Jesus. But Jesus also sanctifies us. He conforms us to his image and sands away the rough edges in our lives. He invites us to join him on his mission.

When we are close to Jesus, that proximity to him is a work that benefits not only us but others as well. When we are close to Jesus, we can bring hope and life and freedom and strength to people trapped in despair and darkness. Jesus has a mission for us, and that's always to draw people one step closer to him. The gospel is not the gospel so we can sit and stare at our navels. The gospel is the gospel because life is short and we have a big God. The gospel is the gospel because Jesus leads us to proclaim the truth that he saves to anybody and everybody on this planet.

Like we talked about earlier, life is short, and God is big, and we need to get into that headspace of knowing that and believing that and saying that and living that. *Life is short. God is big. I'm going to take a step forward. I'm going to obey Christ. I'm not going to be complacent any longer. There's too much work to be done. I'm going to fulfill what I said I would do. Life is short. God is big. I'm going to trust him to do what only he can do.*

6. Keep your guard up.

Goliath had brothers. It was true for David, and it's true for us. There are giants all throughout the land. We don't need to be afraid. We just need to stay vigilant.

When we start to see the fear or the anger or the addiction leave our lives, there can be a void created. The result is twofold: we rid our lives of a giant, and we fill the void with something good. Ultimately, the thing that fills our lives is not a "what" but a "who"—the person and work of Jesus. He is the anchor for our souls, and that anchor rests at the cross of Christ.

Even when we walk closely with Christ, chaos can still throw rocks at us. Painful circumstances can appear in a flash. Jesus never promises us a problem-free life. Yes, there is still the valley of the shadow of death, and yes, there is still the presence of enemies. But thank God, Jesus leads us through the valley. Jesus prepares a table before us in the presence of our enemies. When chaos happens, we're tempted to run away from God. We wonder why bad things continue to happen to us. Yet the call is always to look at the cross. We don't come to believe in God's love for us because of the circumstances around us. We are assured of his love for us because of the circumstance of Christ on the cross. We remind ourselves that the pinnacle and depth and breadth of all chaos was thrown at Jesus. Jesus knows all about suffering. He knows all about pain. He knows all about loss. He was mistreated. He was abused. He was rejected. He suffered death. So we always keep our eyes on Jesus. We deliberately set him always before us.

Author and English evangelist F. B. Meyer wrote,

> I do not believe in sanctification, I believe in the Sanctifier. I do not believe in holiness. I believe in the Holy One. Not an "it," but a Person. Not an attribute, but Christ in my heart. Abide in Jesus. Let the Holy [Spirit] in you keep you abiding in Jesus, so that when Satan comes to knock at your door, Jesus will go and open it, and as soon as the devil sees the face of Christ looking through the door, he will turn tail.[1]

Within that, there might be specific things within the work of Jesus that become part of the exchange.

Let's say your familiar giant is the addiction of overeating. If you feel chaos in your life, then you run to food. As Jesus works in your life and the giant of overeating falls, then you will still be tempted to run to something. Jesus invites you to run to him. Ask Jesus to put something new in your life in exchange for the food. I don't mean you simply swap addictions. I mean you replace the negative with something positive. Maybe you run to a familiar passage of Scripture that you take comfort in. Or maybe you simply go for a walk around your neighborhood; you spend that time walking and talking in intimacy with Christ, telling him how you feel, casting your cares upon him, allowing his Holy Spirit to minister to your heart and mind.

Will there be lapses? Maybe. Your giant is dead, but just like those snake bodies, they might wriggle from time to time. Lapses can be part of the discipleship process. We don't ever need to make excuses for them, but the pattern of repeatedly needed grace is shown in Scripture, even if we closely walk with Jesus. Sometimes Jesus' healing work in our lives is instant and total. But at other times it's a process. Grace abounds. Repent, and God will always forgive. Then get back on track in your relationship with God.

Come to the Table

Let me close this chapter by inviting you to sit with Jesus at a table for two. I want to give you one specific directive. It's this: immerse yourself in Psalm 23, and do this for forty mornings and forty evenings. You can do this directly by reading a Bible, or by reading or listening to the passage on a computer, tablet, or smartphone.

If you want to use your Bible, just turn to the passage and begin to read, morning and evening, first and last thing you do every day.

If you'd rather use your computer, tablet, or smartphone, there's a free app called YouVersion (youversion.com) that lets you download a free version of the Bible, both to read and to listen to. The app is easy to use. You can just pull up Psalm 23, and a nice gentleman reads the psalm to you in a distinguished voice. However you choose to access the words, let them wash over you again and again.

The LORD is my shepherd, I lack nothing.
He makes me lie down in green pastures,
he leads me beside quiet waters,
he refreshes my soul.
He guides me along the right paths
for his name's sake.
Even though I walk
through the darkest valley,
I will fear no evil,
for you are with me;
your rod and your staff,
they comfort me.
You prepare a table before me
in the presence of my enemies.
You anoint my head with oil;
my cup overflows.
Surely your goodness and love will follow me
all the days of my life,
and I will dwell in the house of the LORD
forever.

God is with us, so we lack nothing. He guides us in good directions. He heals us and restores us. He shows us the path that's far away from harmful living. Our freedom and his fame are closely intertwined. God comforts us. Ultimately, all is safe— even if we're walking through a dark valley. We are surrounded in his goodness and mercy all the days of our lives. Ultimately, we'll dwell in the house of the Lord forever.

First thing in the morning, last thing before you go to bed at night, fill your mind and heart with these words. Make this a habit. Don't tap on your messages icon, or your e-mail icon, or your favorite social media icon, or your to-do list, or the weather forecast, or the news. Tap on YouVersion or just leave it open to Psalm 23. Tap on the little speaker icon and if you're alone you can just let it play. If you're married you might want to put your earphones on. Or you might want to listen to it together. Or keep a bookmark in your Bible at this passage, so all you have to do is open it and read.

Here's the rhythm. First thing in the morning, last thing before you go to bed, you seek the face of the Lord through his Word. You say, "Tell me, Lord Jesus, about who you are, about where you lead me, about what my future is. Let me know of your goodness." You wake up, and say, "Tell me again." You may need a break in the middle of the day, so you get up from your cubicle, go in the bathroom, and say, "Tell me again." You may need encouragement when you're in your car, so you say, "Tell me again." Ready for bed: "Tell me again." Your giant wakes you up in the middle of the night: "Tell me again."

For forty mornings and forty evenings you let the Shepherd speak over you, saying, *I sent a teenaged shepherd to take down Goliath, and I am your Shepherd today. I'm standing over your bed tonight. I'm standing in your storm today. I am right here with you in the middle of this valley of the shadow of death right now. It may be darkness all around, but I'm preparing a table before you so that you will have what you need in the midst of the storm. I am with you, and my rod and my staff, they will protect and guide you. I am able and I am here and I am good.*

When you immerse yourself in truth like that, it will drown out any taunts you hear. Filled with truth, you will override the message that your giants have conditioned you to believe. You will say goodbye to the past, and maybe a family bloodline where everybody listened to the giants all their lives. And you will say hello to the fact that you are a son or daughter of almighty God.

Jesus is the Word of God. He is the truth that sets you free. And he is inviting you into his finished work today. "It is for freedom that Christ has set us free. Stand firm, then, and do not let yourselves be burdened again by a yoke of slavery" (Galatians 5:1).

Jesus has won your fight. Your giant is no longer your master. You are free to follow Jesus and experience him in ways you never have before.

Now, for the fuel that powers sustainable change.

CHAPTER 9

Fuel for the Fight

—

If you've been keeping track of the twists and turns in this book, we started by touching upon one big twist. In the story of David and Goliath, we are not David; Jesus is David. We unpacked that twist in depth near the beginning of the book.

Then we looked at a second twist, that our giant is already dead. The victory is already won. Jesus has accomplished what he set out to do. We have unpacked that twist throughout the whole book as we've looked at various specific giants.

As we close this book, we want to look at one final twist, and we've touched upon it in several places already. It's that David's motivation in this whole thing was the fame of God. David was motivated by God's honor and glory. That's our invitation as well.

Very feasibly, David could have hiked up to the battle front, seen Goliath throw down his taunts, and then turned around and hiked straight back home again. David's life wasn't threatened—not at first anyway. He was just delivering supplies. He could've said, "Oh my word, how tall is that guy? Nine feet tall? I've never seen anybody that tall before. He looks intimidating. I'm out of here. I'm heading back down to Dad. I've delivered the food. It's in your tents. I'm checking out. See you later." David wouldn't have been labeled a coward. He wouldn't have been seen as dishonorable. He would've done what a lot of people would have done—ignore the problem and walk away.

Yet that's not what David did.

Why?

David was motivated by something far greater that compelled him to take action—and we're invited to climb into this same headspace right now. What motivated David was that this giant was cursing the God of the army of Israel. David said, "Oh, whoa. Wait a minute, Goliath. All that other stuff you're saying. Maybe. But when you start talking about my God, then we're not tolerating that today. You're going to stop taunting my God right here and now and you're going down. In fact, you *must* go down because God's glory is what we're all about."

This is very important for us to see. God does want us to be free. If there's something that is choking the breath out of our lives, then God wants that stronghold broken. That is what deliverance is all about. Yet deliverance is about more than our freedom. God alone does the work to free us, but in setting us free the aim is that much glory is given to God. That's the truth I want to leave reverberating in your heart as we close this book. Jesus wants to take down our giants so we can walk free and have the life that he wants us to live. And he wants to do that so his name can be exalted above every other name in our world. That's the reason that surpasses all other reasons. It's so people around us look at our lives and say, "Your God is truly God."

Our freedom and God's glory are inextricably woven together. Jesus gave his life on a cross to set us free. He also gave his life on a cross to glorify God. When Jesus went to stretch out his arms, he wasn't just saying, "I want Louie to be free. This is all about Louie. I want Louie to have a wonderful and abundant life. That's why I'm taking sin and death and hell for all mankind."

No. Jesus was saying, "See this, Louie, you're about to get swept up into something amazing right here, because all your chains are about to be broken. They're going to be broken so people will know that the God of Israel is the one true God. There is no God like him in this world. He is the God of mercy, kindness, grace, compassion, and love. He is the God who does not hold our sins against us. God is just—and he's also the *Justifier*. God both offers his Son as a substitute and a sacrifice so that then he can be just, but then God also justifies all of us who went wrong. No other god is going to do that. No other god is going to enter humanity. No other god will humble himself and come to earth to be born a baby because he loves us so much. But the God who is the God alone in the heavens will do that. So here I go, Father. I'm going to set Louie free, and I'm going to set all people free, but ultimately this is all for you. This is for your glory. This is to show the world how amazing you are. You are the Lord, and there is no other."

Grasping this two-fold motivator is important: Jesus stretched out his arms on the cross both to free us and to glorify God. Both of those works happened at the same time. They're woven together, and one is important, yet the other one always carries more weight. As long as our motivation remains only about getting freedom for ourselves, then we're missing what's most important, and we won't truly have the full power to change. God wants to open our eyes to this understanding. We're fighting for our freedom, and we're also fighting for his glory. When we do that we agree with God. We say, "God, I want to be free. You know I desperately want to be free. But I also want you to be glorified, because not only is this giant demoralizing me, but this thing is diminishing your glory. It's telling people every day that my God isn't big enough. My God isn't powerful enough. My God doesn't have the right stuff for me to be free."

One of the greatest concerns of the modern Christian is the tendency to make everything about us. We reduce Jesus to a self-improvement technique, saying, "He helps me feel better about my life." The same happens with our relationship with church. You hear people say, "I got a lot out of that." Or, "I like that

Our lives' central aim is to *enjoy* this great God and to *glorify* him forever.

church because it helps me." In the end, the person of Christ, the promise of the Word, the gathering of the people, the work of the cross, the hope of heaven, all become about "me."

God wants you to experience the fullness of everything he has accomplished for you and all of who he is, but it's not all about you. God does not exist for us; we exist for God. We are not his maker, he is our Maker. Our lives' central aim is to enjoy this great God and to glorify him forever.

One of the ways we glorify God best is by experiencing his victory against the giants that come against us. In so doing, our motivation isn't all about self-improvement; that's just the benefit. Our motivation comes in realizing that every giant that defeats us deflates our ability to make much of Jesus to the world. There's an extra motivation in our hearts when we say, "This Goliath, it must go down, God, because you must be lifted high."

This is one of the keys in battling giants. We talk to our giant about the fame of God. The conversation is not, "Hey, you're bothering me. You're annoying me. You're sucking the life out of me. You're strangling me." Instead, it's, "Hey, you're robbing God, and I can't tolerate that. When your taunts were just about me, that was one thing. But now I realize these taunts are about my God, and that's something else altogether. If you talk bad about my God, then you gotta go down, giant. For the sake of the name of the Great King, you're going down today!"

Made for Greater Glory

With all this *glory talk* flying, it might be helpful to take a step back so you can better see you were wired for something more. None of us arrived on the planet without divine assistance. We didn't make ourselves; we were created by a higher power, a divine source, Jesus himself. We are designed to be dependent on our Creator and reflective of his greatness and glory. We get life and breath and gifts and opportunities, and God gets credit and glory and praise from our lives.

This is what we are made for. That's why glory is woven through every fiber of our being.

Maybe you're not highly motivated by God's glory just yet, certainly not enough to walk into the Valley of Elah and take down Goliath, but there is some glory fueling everything about you right now.

I was raised on Auburn football. There really wasn't much of a choice in our household, as my dad had graduated from there in 1957, a football championship year! My earliest memories of college football are of my sister, dad, and me listening to Auburn games on the radio and watching my dad running toward the giant stereo system he had built and yelling into the speakers as if everyone could hear him. When Auburn made a game-winning play, you would find all three of us bounding from one piece of furniture to the next, dancing on the sofa and the coffee table, screaming our heads off.

After my dad died in the spring one year, I wanted to make the trip to Auburn with my mom that fall to see a game together, a special outing to remember Dad. We arrived on campus to a tumultuous downpour and were not prepared. We knew the forecast had called for a shower here or there, but this was a deluge. Out of options, I think we bought trash bags at the local supermarket, cut holes in them, and wore them like ponchos as we began our mile-long walk toward the stadium. (When I say downpour, think Noah's flood. It was raining so hard we couldn't hear ourselves talk.)

You'd think no one would show up in this weather, but you'd be wrong. Auburn-wrong. Once we shuffled to our upper-deck seats it was still almost an hour until kickoff, but the stadium was nearly full. It didn't hurt that we were playing a dreaded conference rival who, at the time, was the number one ranked team.

Close to eighty thousand of us were clamoring in the rain-soaked moment. A buzz was in the air. Auburn cheerleaders started a chant. On the opposite side of the stadium they held up signs toward the crowd, which was followed by a loud and determined shout now headed toward us—*O R A N G E!*

Quickly the other half of the cheer squad raised before us signs reading *B L U E!*

And so it began. For maybe five minutes this continued, with each successive wave getting louder than the previous one.

ORANGE!

BLUE!

At one point during our side's reply, I looked over at my sixty-five-year-old mom. Her hair (oh my, she'd hate me saying this, even though she's in heaven) was plastered to her head as if she were standing in the shower. The veins were sticking out on the side of her neck. Then, as if she were going to single-handedly drown out the forty thousand people across from us, she took a huge breath. Her eyes were bulging dangerously from her eye sockets as she screamed with a force I thought might level her—a deep, guttural, rattling, scary scream—

BLUUUUUUUUUUUUUUUE!

Man!

There we were, in a driving rain, losing our minds, yelling like we'd been set on fire. Why? So we could amplify *two colors*, the colors that represent our beloved Auburn.

That, my friends, is glory. Not ultimate glory, mind you. But glory for sure.

I left that day wondering what it would be like to live like that for God's fame.

For you, the colors might be different, but if you think about it, you're most likely screaming into the rain about something or someone. Glory is a part of who we are. It's what we are made for. The game-changing shift comes when we see that God's glory is unrivaled and unending glory, and we begin to shape our days around the decisions that will bring praise to him in all we do.

The Heart of David, a Heart for God

In the ancient Old Testament narrative, the ark of the Lord was the most treasured possession of God's people, the embodiment of his very presence and glory among them. You can check out the whole story in three passages: 1 Samuel 4:1–7:1, 2 Samuel 6, and 1 Chronicles 15–16.

The Israelites were in battle with the Philistines again, although it was a different time than the David and Goliath encounter. The battle wasn't going well for the Israelites. The two armies came out and had a major collision in combat, and it looked like the people of God were going to get wiped out. So the priests went back up to the place of worship and got the ark of the covenant and brought it down to the battlefield as if to say, "Hey, we're bringing God's presence down here and we're going to kick y'all all the way back up to where you came from. Now we got the holy ark of the covenant and the presence of God, and we can't be beat."

When the ark came down, the Israelites let loose with this huge roar, and the Philistines were like, "Uh-oh, this could be trouble. We've heard about this ark. We're doomed. Who will deliver us from the hand of these mighty gods? They're the same gods who struck the Egyptians with all kinds of plagues in the wilderness. Be strong, Philistines! Be men and fight!"

But God wasn't in on the plan, because the hearts of the

Israelites who called for the ark were wicked. The Philistines fought hard, and God let the Israelites fall prey to the hands of the Philistines that day. Not only did much of the Israelite army get destroyed, but the Philistines stole the ark of the covenant of God. They carted it back to their city of Ashdod in Philistia and placed it in the temple of their god, Dagon, a tall, stone idol. They did this to taunt the Israelites. It was a way of saying, "Ha-ha. There you are, nice little shiny ark of the covenant with your cherubim and all your beautiful glory. Look—we've got Dagon, and Dagon is amazing."

Here's what happened. The Philistines all went home to party that night after thinking they'd showed whose god was who. But when they came back the next morning, their god had fallen over facedown in front of the ark of the covenant of God. *Hello? How'd that happen?* None of the Philistines could figure it out. So they spent a day propping Dagon back up. Once that was done, they figured all was well and went off to party again. The next morning, same thing. They came back, and Dagon was on the ground again, lying flat before the ark of God. This time Dagon's head and his hands were broken off. The Philistines were baffled. Who has a rock cutter around here? Who shows up in the night and cuts the head and hands off our god? To add insult to injury, the head and the hands were piled up on the threshold of the doorway. On arrival, the Philistines had to step over their damaged, broken-down god as they entered into the temple.

You know why the Philistine's god was toppled? Because God

is serious about his glory. When there was nobody to defend his glory, God defended it himself. Don't you love that? God was like, *Oh, so you're going to put me in here with that piece of stone? I will turn Dagon into powder. I will grind your tiny god into pea gravel. You can put him in the bottom of your aquarium. Oh, you're propping up your god again after I pushed him over? No problem, Philistines. I'll take this as far as you want to go. Understand that I am the Lord. I am God—period. I will not give my glory to another god or share any of my praise with false idols. I won't sit here and be taunted by a rock. I don't care how tall the statue of your Dagon is; it must go down.*

Finally, the Philistines clued in and returned the ark of God to Israel.

Sadly, the Israelites had again forgotten about the dangerous beauty of the glory of God. When they got it back they'd forgotten how to properly carry the ark and lives were lost. Exasperated, David said, "How can the ark of the LORD ever come to me?" (2 Samuel 6:9). After several failed and disastrous attempts to bring the ark to Jerusalem, King David finally had the ark brought to the city on poles, as God had instructed in the first place. Even then the journey was no small matter.

Once the ark was being carried properly, the journey to Jerusalem resumed safely. David and his men were so grateful. They were so happy to be alive in the presence of such glory that they took six steps, then built an altar and offered a sacrifice of praise to God! They were humbled and amazed in the presence of a holy God. Then they took another six steps, then built another altar and offered another sacrifice of praise to God. That's how they moved—in constant worship—all the way to the ark's destination.

David had a heart that longed for God's righteousness. He had that motivation in his life. He desired God's glory above his own. Remember what David said to Goliath just before Goliath went down. Look again at 1 Samuel 17:45–47:

> David said to the Philistine, "You come against me with sword and spear and javelin, but I come against you in the name of the LORD Almighty, the God of the armies of Israel, whom you have defied. This day the LORD will deliver you into my hands, and I'll strike you down and cut off your head. This very day I will give the carcasses of the Philistine army to the birds and the wild animals, and the whole world will know that there is a God in Israel. All those gathered here will know that it is not by sword or spear that the LORD saves; for the battle is the LORD's, and he will give all of you into our hands."

Note the progression. The first thing David said to Goliath was, "Hey, you're going down. One giant is definitely going down today, Goliath, and it's going to be you." Then David, in the power of God, looked up on the hillside and said, "And all the rest of you are going down with him! Anyone here who's taunting God's people, who's debilitating the work of God, is going down." Then David spoke about the ultimate reason behind it all. "You're going down so the whole world will know that there is a God in Israel. All those gathered here will know that it is not by sword or spear that the Lord saves; for the battle is the Lord's, and he will give all of you into our hands."

We know the rest of the story. David took his sling and with one rock silenced the giant. The stone sank into the forehead of Goliath and cracked into his skull and knocked him dead and he fell over. Done. The word of God went out over the whole valley of Elah. "There is a God, and he is the God of Israel. He is the one true God. Goliath has fallen. The enemy is gone. Victory is ours!"

Our boy David brings it all home for us. He was a shepherd boy who fell in love with the God of wonder beyond our galaxy. He was the teen who faced down the dreaded Philistine giant. And he was the man after God's own heart who, at all costs, returned the presence of God (the ark) to the people of God in the city of God. But David would have understood the scene in that driving rainstorm at Jordan-Hare Stadium as well. For it was David who prompts us to live lives that really matter in Psalm 145:

> Great is the LORD and most worthy of praise;
>> his greatness no one can fathom.
> One generation commends your works to another;
>> they tell of your mighty acts.
> They speak of the glorious splendor of your majesty—
>> and I will meditate on your wonderful works.

They tell of the power of your awesome works—
and I will proclaim your great deeds.
They celebrate your abundant goodness
and joyfully sing of your righteousness. (vv. 3–7)

As he continues, we see the fire that fueled his fight:

The LORD is gracious and compassionate,
slow to anger and rich in love.
The LORD is good to all;
he has compassion on all he has made.
All your works praise you, LORD;
your faithful people extol you.
They tell of the glory of your kingdom
and speak of your might,
so that all people may know of your mighty acts
and the glorious splendor of your kingdom.
Your kingdom is an everlasting kingdom,
and your dominion endures through all generations.
The LORD is trustworthy in all he promises
and faithful in all he does.
The LORD upholds all who fall
and lifts up all who are bowed down.
The eyes of all look to you,
and you give them their food at the proper time.
You open your hand
and satisfy the desires of every living thing.

The LORD is righteous in all his ways
  and faithful in all he does.
The LORD is near to all who call on him,
  to all who call on him in truth.
He fulfills the desires of those who fear him;
  he hears their cry and saves them.
The LORD watches over all who love him,
  but all the wicked he will destroy.
My mouth will speak in praise of the LORD.
  Let every creature praise his holy name
  for ever and ever. (vv. 8–21)

From the east let us lift a shout of praise to his holy name. And from the west let us echo, "The Lord is good." From the south let the older generation say, "He is faithful and true." From the north let the young reply, "Our God is the mighty God who saves."

Our giants are dead, and our God is on his throne.

Out of the Ashes, Glory

———

Billy Graham told how once in Scotland, some sport fishermen spent the day fishing, then that evening went to an inn for dinner. One of the fishermen, in describing the size of the fish that got away, threw open his arms just as a waitress passed by with a tea pot. The man's arm hit the pot, and rich, dark tea splashed against the wall, leaving an ugly brown stain. Greatly embarrassed, the man jumped up and apologized profusely, but right at that moment another of the inn's guests jumped up and said, "Never mind."

The guest pulled a marker from his pocket and began to sketch around the stain. Soon a picture emerged. A magnificent royal stag with his antlers spread. All the inn's guests gathered around to admire the work. They soon realized that the sketch artist was none other than Sir Edwin Landseer, Great Britain's foremost painter of animals. What had begun as a stain had been transformed into beautiful art.

Billy Graham wrote, "This story has always beautifully illustrated to me that fact that if we confess not only our sins but our mistakes to God, He can make out of them something for our good and for His glory."[1]

All of us have fallen short of our best hopes for our lives. Our choices have disappointed ourselves and those around us. But God is uniquely skilled to take the mistakes of our lives and turn them into something beautiful that brings him praise. As we look across our Valley of Elah, we see our foes taunting us and seeking to steal God's glory.

But a victor has emerged in our story and he is sitting with you right now as you come to the finish of this book. His name is Jesus, and he takes down the giants and announces freedom for us all. He sees the stain and the pain you have endured. He knows the "less" you have grown accustomed to and is still committed to leading you into his best.

I don't want you to close this book and think Jesus is asking you to "try harder." No, he's not asking you to make everything new on your own. He is simply asking you to see him—to see the work he has done for you and to believe again that he can raise any of us from the ashes of defeat.

Jesus is inviting us to set our attention on him and to rest in his grace. Follow him in this moment with your next step. And keep on doing that step after step today. If you do, his glory will ultimately result.

Goliath must fall. Your goliath must fall. Your giant must fall because Jesus is already victorious.

Now is the time to walk in the freedom that he has won.

Acknowledgments

We call our church a House, because church can often denote a building or organization while *House* reflects what we truly are, a family. When something happens in our Passion City Church house (or your house), everyone, in some way, shares the credit. This book is no different.

Simply put, no one ever writes alone. Even a solitary writer shuttered in the hills for months writing in isolation has been birthed, shaped, and inspired by someone or something beyond his or her doing.

Goliath Must Fall is inspired by a series of messages that came to life at Passion City Church. The truths of this book resonated powerfully in our lives, helping us make shifts in our thinking and in the way we identify ourselves in the beloved story of David and Goliath, which provides the backdrop for this book.

While the messages were in existence, the book you are

holding was made possible by the skill and craft of my friend, Marcus Brotherton, an accomplished and awarded author with a heart for Christ and his church. Marcus worked through the transcripts of the original messages and made notes from our lengthy conversations in order to orchestrate the initial framework for the book. His input throughout was not only insightful, but useful, in making this project the best it could be.

Writing a book, while living life, is a process that requires incredible partnerships. I have been extraordinarily blessed with the best partner anyone could imagine—my wife Shelley, the love of my life. Her faith, brilliance, discernment, servant-heart, and devotion are reflected on every page. She always cheers me on, makes way for the hours it takes to craft a work like this, and provides the best kind of feedback—the honest kind. I am far better because of her. The same can be said for this book.

Kevin Marks, my friend and the head of our Passion Publishing venture, has steered this journey with exceptional wisdom and patience. Few book projects happen on schedule and this one is no exception. Yet Kevin has kept us headed in the right direction and made it possible for us to arrive at what we believe is a helpful destination for everyone who reads *Goliath Must Fall*. His teammate, Alissa Roberts, cares about each resource as if it were her own, helping the world find and connect with the words and truths inside.

The team at W Publishing Group, led by Matt Baugher, has been an exceptional partner.

My team at home is remarkable in every way. Sue Graddy, Anna Butel, and Christina Schubert help keep everything moving in a positive direction and have given their energy and passion to help *Goliath Must Fall* become a reality. Meghan Brim did a beautiful job with the cover design and inside layout, with help and input from the incomparable Leighton Ching.

If any of our giants are going down, it's all because of Jesus. He is the giant-slayer. It's not a young boy with a slingshot that's the hero of this story (our story), but a Savior wrapped in human skin dying to defeat everything that tried to take our lives. Our hope is that in these pages he will be seen, savored, and adored.

I love you, Jesus.

Notes

Chapter 2: Dead but Still Deadly

1. Lauren Chandler, "5 Misconceptions About the Pastor's Wife," The Gospel Coalition, October 14, 2015, https://www.thegospelcoalition.org/article/5-misconceptions-about-the-pastors-wife, reprinted with permission from Crossway, "Pastors' Wives: 5 Misconceptions," March 24, 2015, https://www.crossway.org/blog/2015/03/pastors-wives-5-misconceptions-2/.

2. A. T. Pierson, *The Gospel: Its Heart, Heights, and Hopes*, vol. 1 (Grand Rapids, MI: Baker Book House, 1978), 220, 234.

Chapter 6: Anger Must Fall

1. J. I. Packer, *Knowing God* (Downers Grove, IL: Inter-Varsity Press, 1973), 134.

Chapter 8: A Table in the Presence

1. F. B. Meyer, *The Christ Life for Your Life* (Chicago: Moody Press, n.d.), 66, 72.

Chapter 9: Fuel for the Fight

1. Billy Graham, *How to Be Born Again* (Waco, TX: Word, 1977), 129–30.

About the Author

Louie Giglio is pastor of Passion City Church and the founder of the Passion movement, which exists to call a generation to leverage their lives for the fame of Jesus.

Since 1997, Passion has gathered collegiate-aged young people in events across the U.S. and around the world. Most recently, Passion 2017 gathered more than 55,000 students in Atlanta's Georgia Dome in one of the largest collegiate gatherings in its history.

In addition to the collegiate gatherings of Passion Conferences, Louie and his wife Shelley lead the teams at Passion City Church, sixstepsrecords, and the Passion Global Institute.

Louie is the author of *The Comeback, The Air I Breathe, I Am Not But I Know I Am*, and *Goliath Must Fall*. As a communicator, Louie speaks at events throughout the U.S. and across the globe. He is widely known for messages like "Indescribable" and "How Great Is Our God."

An Atlanta native and graduate of Georgia State University, Louie has done postgraduate work at Baylor University and holds a master's degree from Southwestern Baptist Theological Seminary. Louie and Shelley make their home in Atlanta.

It's Not the Height of the Giant ...but the Size of Our God

EXPLORE THE PRINCIPLES IN *GOLIATH MUST FALL* WITH YOUR small group through this six-session video-based study. Each week, pastor Louie Giglio will provide practical steps and biblical principles for how you and your group can defeat the "giants" in your lives like fear, rejection, comfort, anger, or addiction. Includes discussion questions, Bible exploration, and personal study materials for in between sessions.

9780718088866-A